...re the outbreak of the American Revolution, a frail, twelve-year-old boy boarded an English ship to begin a career in the British Navy, a career in which he would distinguish himself and be called Britain's greatest naval hero.

Whether aboard a frigate, a ship of the line, or a converted merchantman, hardship and peril were part of a day's work at sea in those days of sailing ships.

Horatio Nelson was a man of indomitable spirit who grew in stature as a naval strategist until, among other things, he kept Napoleon from gaining control of the Channel and making England a province of France.

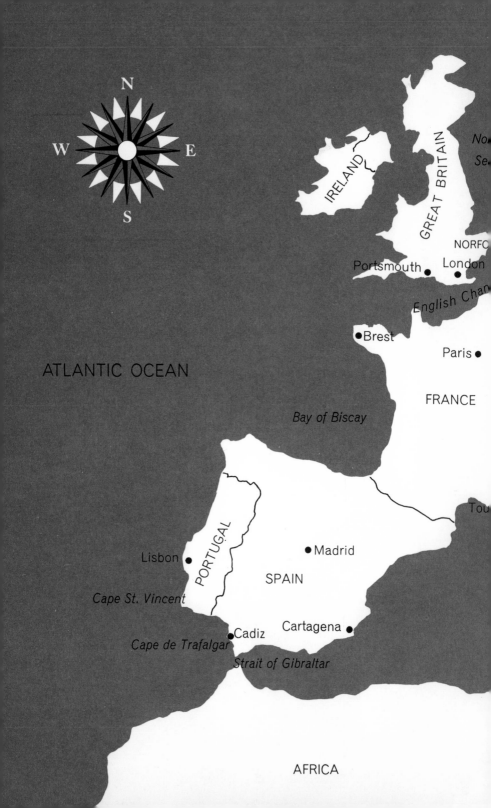

the true story of

LORD NELSON

the true story of

LORD
NELSON

NAVAL HERO

BY RICHARD HOUGHTON

CHILDRENS PRESS, CHICAGO

H—6

American edition published through the courtesy of

Frederick Muller Limited

London

Library of Congress Catalog Card Number: 64-12908

Copyright © in Great Britain, 1958, Richard Houghton

© 1964, Childrens Press

Lithographed in the U.S.A.

Contents

Foreword

Twelve-year-old Midshipman 15

The West Indies and Trouble 27

Black Days in the Mediterranean 39

Nelson Insures a Victory 53

Disaster and Futile Search 61

Fighting Stations, Aboukir Bay 79

Cautious Approach to Copenhagen 91

Gun Duel in the Baltic 99

Weary Sea Chase 113

Hero of Trafalgar 125

Index of Place Names 140

Foreword

A few years before the outbreak of the American Revolution, a frail, twelve-year-old boy boarded an English ship to begin a career in the British Navy, a career in which he would distinguish himself and be called Britain's greatest naval hero.

Whether aboard a frigate, a ship of the line, or a converted merchantman, hardship and peril were part of a day's work at sea in those days of sailing ships.

Horatio Nelson was a man of indomitable spirit who grew in stature as a naval strategist until, among other things, he kept Napoleon from gaining control of the Channel and making England a province of France.

Credits

Designer/BERT RAY STUDIO

Illustrations by/PARVIZ SADIGHIAN

Cover Painting/MARY GEHR

Type/CALEDONIA

Paper/ 70# PUBLISHERS OFFSET

Printer/REGENSTEINER CORPORATION

Artist

Parviz Sadighian was born in Tehran, Iran, in 1939. He was graduated from the Academy of Fine Arts in Tehran and received a partial scholarship for foreign study. In 1959 he enrolled at the Art Institute in Chicago and continued his studies in sculpture and in painting. Interest in painting led to courses in illustration and advertising art. Mr. Sadighian is now associated with the Bert Ray Studio in Chicago.

Twelve-Year-Old Midshipman

At the end of 1770 a naval captain, so well dressed that his nickname was "Fine Bones," sat in his cabin in a 64-gun ship in the Medway, staring disbelievingly at a letter he had just received. And then he laughed. It was absurd. That his skinny little twelve-year-old nephew, who was always ailing, should ask his father to beg him a place in the ship—that was truly incredible.

Eventually the captain roused himself, and took pen and paper. He was a good-natured enough man in his careless way, and did not wish to disoblige his brother-in-law who, he knew, found it difficult to make both ends meet, with a large family to provide for; on the other hand, he could not, for the life of him, conceal his surprise that this particular nephew above all should want to come to sea—nor, because he was so certain that this nephew was absolutely unsuited to a naval career, welcome him in anything but a distinctly unflattering and lukewarm manner.

"What has poor Horace done, who is so weak, that he above all the rest should be sent to rough it out at sea?" he demanded. "But let him come; and the first time we go into action, a cannon ball may knock off his head, and provide for him at once."

So wrote Captain Suckling, very hastily—then he went back to what he felt were far more pressing matters, never knowing that he had just written the most important document in all the history of the Royal Navy.

Now what exactly did the captain know of Horace, and Horace's family, to leave him quite stupefied by the information that Horace "above all the rest" wanted to be a sailor?

In the first place, the Nelson children were nearly all delicate—three of the little boys had died in babyhood. Life in a King's ship was not the life for any delicate child, least of all for Horace, who was always having ague, or catching colds, or suffering agonies from toothache, or being made sick by the smell of paint.

In the second place, no one had ever heard of a *Nelson* in the Navy; the family was one of complete landlubbers, whose boys nearly always entered the Church. So why on earth should Horace, most delicate of the children still living, want to go to sea? He would undoubtedly be horribly seasick, for a start! (And indeed he was—dreadfully seasick, even when he became commander-in-chief of the Mediterranean Fleet, just as, to be completely unheroic, one might say, he was suffering torments from toothache when he won his first great victory.)

All in all, Captain Suckling felt his nephew would be as helpless in a ship at sea as a fish out of water on land.

And why, we can imagine him asking himself in exasperation, did the confounded boy *want* to come?

This was a question that Horace (or Horatio) Nelson himself might have found difficult to answer; he only knew he *must* go. Partly, of course, it must have been the influence of his mother, dead these three years—Horatio's sister recalled that she was a "heroine for the sailors," and Horatio (Horace was the form used only by members of his family) himself remembered that she hated the French. Did she, sister of a naval officer, tell her small son stories of the sea, so that Captain "Fine Bones" Suckling was the hero of his childhood? Certainly October 21 was a day to be celebrated in the Nelson family, for on that day, in 1759, the captain's *Dreadnought,* with two other vessels, had engaged a much larger French squadron in the West Indies, as Horatio was to recall forty-six years later, on the eve of an infinitely greater October 21.

Yet this alone does not seem sufficient to answer the question of why Horatio Nelson uprooted himself at the age of twelve from familiar surroundings to go off to face the unknown. Perhaps the real answer lies in his name—Nelson. It is a Scandinavian name, and there can be no doubt that this most fragile of sailors was descended from those fair-headed, fearless giants, the Vikings, who were the greatest sailors the world has ever known, taking their longboats from the misty northern fiords into the glare of the Mediterranean, to Iceland and Greenland, across the grey Atlantic waters centuries before Columbus made his "discovery" of America—and, of course, coming to England, first to fight, then to settle in the east and the north. It was not for nothing

17

that Nelson one day wrote a letter addressed to "the *brothers of Englishmen, the Danes.*"

So I believe that in 1770 something stirred in the blood of a delicate boy of twelve, something that he could not understand; but his tall Norse ancestors would have known this tug of the sea, the whale road, the gulls' way, the magic made up of wind and wave and the cry of seabirds, and I think too that the same fierce ancestors must have given grim smiles of approval when, in the years to come, their descendant described the thick of a murderous battle as "the full tide of happiness."

But if the sea called to him because his ancestors had fought it and loved it a thousand years before, it was through a more immediate relative that he was able to answer that call—through Captain Suckling, who agreed to take his nephew into his ship, who had him rated in the books of the *Raisonnable* from January 1, 1771, who sent for him in March when the ship at last was ready . . .

And then coolly went off on leave, without thinking to tell anyone that his nephew was coming.

The occasion that most severely tested the courage of Horatio Nelson came at the very beginning of his naval career—on the day he first joined his ship. Going to a new school at the age of twelve is bad enough, in all conscience, but any boy joining the Navy had to accept in his heart that he would have to face and live through ordeals a landsman could never dream of. He would have to take peril and hardship in his stride—it was all part of the day's work in the Navy, and soon accepting danger and discomfort would simply be part of one's duty within the walls of this harsh wooden world, a world which was a byword for brutality even in those rough days, a world where white-faced homesick children, terribly lonely, were forced to become men over night. But we cannot doubt that young Nelson thought that he would be luckier than most, for would not his own uncle be there to greet and guide him?

So, comforted by this thought, he was able to say farewell with fair composure to his brother and schoolfellow, William, when the familiar figure of his father's servant, Peter, appeared in the chill and gloom of an early spring morning to escort him to the Lynn carriage, where his father was waiting to accompany him to London. But he must make the journey from London to Chatham—and the infinitely greater journey beyond—alone. He was a man now.

The stagecoach set him down at Chatham; the other passengers left him, some being met by friends or relations, the others setting out with purposeful strides for a destination they knew. But there was no one to meet Horatio Nelson, and after waiting for some time he realized he must find his own way to his ship. She was lying in the Medway, he knew that much; then he must find his way to the busy river, and get aboard her.

Cold and hungry, tired and—yes, Nelson was frightened, too—he managed to make his way through the jostling crowds and came to where the ships of the line lay. Yet even when he eventually found his uncle's ship, he could not find anyone who would take him out to her.

He wandered about in the cold, not knowing where to turn, until a naval officer, whose name we do not know, stopped the forlorn little figure and asked him what he was doing. On hearing the explanation, Nelson's new acquaintance invited him to come to his home where he might have something to eat and drink before being set aboard his uncle's ship. When at last this unknown friend sped him on his way, Nelson, who always needed only a little to encourage him, must have thought the worst was over. Once he was aboard his uncle's ship everything would be well, and the miserable hours spent in straying about the quay would be forgotten.

But the nightmare had not ended yet. He boarded the ship, reported himself—only to receive blank looks. Captain Suckling? He was not in the ship, and was not expected for some days. Still, one must remember that a post captain could not be expected to dance attendance on a midshipman, even if that midshipman were his nephew. One must swallow hard, and remember that, and go on to say (praying one's voice did not shake), "Sir, my name is Horatio Nelson, and I have been rated on the books of this ship as midshipman since the first day of January." But they knew nothing of that. Captain Suckling had never mentioned a nephew to anyone; no one expected a midshipman by the name of Nelson.

So one paced the decks alone and in silence for all that remained of that dreadful day . . .

And when night fell on the waters of the Medway?

We can only suppose that he stumbled below, and found some hole where he could creep like a terrified small animal. Did he eat—rather, try to eat—and find his proper berth? It is doubtful, for it was not until the following day that someone took compassion on him—and spoke to him.

So now his troubles were over. He was shown where he would live, sleep, eat and study—the midshipman's berth on the orlop, lowest deck of the ship, a dingy den knowing neither light nor air, reeking with bilge water from the hold below. How much space he might have for himself is uncertain, but some idea may be gained from a letter written by a midshipman in a brig at the time of the war against Napoleon—the boy said, without irony, that they did not have "much room to spare" aboard the *Helicon*, there being "7 of us in a berth 8 feet by 6."

We know nothing of how Nelson managed to survive his first bitter days of service, but that they were days of heartbreak we may guess from certain betraying things he said and did years later to ease the life of midshipmen when *he* was a captain—as his neglectful uncle and first captain assuredly never can have done.

There was, for example, the way in which he helped the boys to overcome the fear any normal person would feel when first required to climb the dizzying height of the masthead—it was, in fact, such an ordeal that "mastheading" was one of the chief punishments a bad captain would inflict on a midshipman. But Nelson was different; a lady who was a passenger in the 28-gun *Boreas*, commanded by him, noticed that if any boy was afraid of first going aloft, the captain—seemingly quite unaware of the boy's piteous state of nerves—would say to him with a smile, "Well, sir, I am going a race to the masthead, and beg that I may meet you there." Then he would go into the ratlines, and so would the boy, of course, to scramble up as best as he could—but here again the captain would seem quite unaware of how slowly or clumsily the ascent was made. Then, when they met in the top, Nelson would talk to the boy in a friendly manner, laughingly remarking after a time how deserving of pity was the poor wretch who fancied that getting up was either dangerous or difficult; and one could almost be certain that when the midshipman readily agreed with his captain (it is usually just as well for a midshipman to agree with his captain) in this case the agreement would be perfectly sincere. After Nelson's treatment, getting up had lost all its terrors.

Each day he would go into the schoolroom, to see that the midshipmen were studying properly, and at noon, he was always first on deck with his quadrant—the elements of navigation, being based on such things as spherical trigonometry, can be hard to master for people without a gift for mathematics, but the captain's constant interest in his midshipmen's progress would put the least mathematical of boys on his mettle. Nor did Nelson lose interest in his "young gentlemen" when his ship was in port—in fact, he made a point of taking his midshipmen ashore and introducing them to his friends. He even took one of them with him to dine with the governor of Barbados, presenting him with these words: "Your Excellency must excuse me for bringing one of my midshipmen. I make it a rule to introduce them to all the good company I can, as they have few to look up to, besides myself, during the time they are at sea."

But most betraying of all is a comment of just three words made by Nelson when he was Commander-in-chief in the Mediterranean. He had invited a midshipman called Parsons to dine with him, and what was more, had had Midshipman Parsons put in the place of honor—at his own right hand. In the course of the conversation, he asked with a smile how old his guest had been on entering the Service. Eleven years old, said Parsons.

Nelson stopped smiling then. As if to himself he whispered, "Much too young."

After six months Captain Suckling became the commander of a guardship lying in the Thames. Since this would not help his nephew's practical education, Nelson for the time being left the Royal Navy, and for the following year he was in a merchant vessel, trading with the West Indies. After this he could proudly claim to be a practical seaman, but his service in a merchant ship had one result that was both unexpected and unpleasant as far as his uncle was concerned—his nephew came back with all the merchant sailor's dislike of the King's service, quoting fervently all the prevailing beliefs about the ordinary seaman being definitely superior to naval officers.

Captain Suckling, appalled by the thought that the docile Horatio might quit the King's for the merchant service—and make his uncle thereby something of a laughingstock—descended to something like bribery. If his nephew would stay, he should go in the cutter attached to the commanding officer's ship at Chatham. . . . So Horatio learned all the arts of the pilot off the Tower and Chatham and the North Foreland, after which shoals and rocks never had any terrors for him. But it had been a near thing, and the history of the world would have been different if the outbreak of the war against France in 1793 had found Nelson in a merchant vessel, instead of being appointed to a sail of the line.

Yet after a few months in his uncle's ship, Nelson, tired of the grey wet mists of the river and being stationed on London's doorstep, was seeking more adventurous employment. It so happened that at this time two naval vessels were being sent on a voyage of exploration to the far north, and Nelson, hearing this, was afire to go on the expedition. Even the discovery that, because of the difficulties and dangers that might arise on such a voyage, it had been decided to take able-bodied men instead of the boys usually serving in a ship, did not daunt him; he tried and tried again until flat refusal became grudging permission, and on June 4, the two ships sailed from the Nore, with Nelson coxswain to Captain Lutwidge, the second-in-command.

At the beginning of August, the expedition faced disaster, for ice held the ships fast.

If they were to escape the ice they would have to *cut* their way out, and this they began to do, sawing through pieces twelve feet thick, but still the ice crept closer, and every hour lessened their chances of escape. Yet young Nelson, ever an optimist, was looking forward to his return home with the skin of a polar bear as a present for his elderly father, *not* protected by nature against the cold . . . and the stone floors of a country rectory . . . and the bitter winds that swept across the North Sea to bite into the bones of Norfolk dwellers. So one night, in the middle watch, he took advantage of the mist to steal from his ship and set off across the ice in pursuit of a bear. He was missed, and Captain Lutwidge, pacing up and down, peering into the ever-thickening fog, became seriously alarmed about him—and also, quite understandably, furious with the truant. Even when the weather cleared between three and four in the morning, and keen eyes saw Nelson at some distance from the ship, the captain's worries were anything but over, for there he was, musket in hand, attacking a bear so huge that it was like a mountain of white fur. Moreover, his musket chose this moment to fail him—it flashed in the pan, but did not fire. Yet this hair-raising situation, far from sending Nelson running for his life, left him with no idea save to get to grips with the growling monster—"Never mind," he called cheerfully, "do but let me get a blow at this devil with the butt end of my musket, and we shall have him." He was always optimistic.

The situation was saved because Captain Lutwidge ordered a gun to be fired, and the bear lumbered away at the sound, leaving Nelson to retrace his steps to the ship, probably gloomily reflecting that he would infinitely prefer to meet any number of angry polar bears to one furious officer in blue and gold, who would not understand about the icy winds and freezing rectory of Burnham Thorpe.

But the chief enemy, of course, threatening all, was ice—and ice could not be frightened away. The expedition knew that if they stayed where they were and the weather did *not* change, not a man would survive the winter, so they began to make plans to abandon ship, hauling the boats over the ice. Then the miracle happened; they got the wind they wanted, and gaps appeared in the ice. Still, it would be foolish to hope too much, so while the ships, with all sails set, groped very slowly to the west—covering only a mile in a day—Nelson and the others already at the job continued hauling the boats over the ice. Then fog fell again, but when the mist lifted this time, the worst was over; the wind was easterly, and the ice was beginning to drift westward with the ships. Soon they were in the open sea again.

At least, there was variety enough in Nelson's early career. Almost immediately after his return to England, he was off on another voyage, in the *Seahorse,* bound for the East Indies. When he set sail, his family might well have congratulated themselves that he had thrown off his early delicacy; he was an active, healthy-looking boy, with a good fresh color. But after eighteen months in India, he fell so ill that he never looked robust again—fever reduced him to a skeleton, paralyzed him for a time, and doctors said his only hope of survival lay in returning home. Even so, he would never have lived through the long voyage round the Cape if it had not been for the care of the captain of the vessel that had brought him back—and sometimes, in the dreadful bleak depression that often follows illness, the sick boy wished they had let him die. He had made good friends in India—especially a gigantic young fellow called Troubridge—and he had left them to pursue their careers with all the blessings of good health, while he himself felt he was finished, for was not his health broken? Lying there in his hot, stuffy cabin, through the sleepless night hours, sometimes he wished himself overboard. But then, patriotism and hopefulness came like a flood of sunshine, driving before it the darkness of doubt and misery. *He would be a hero*—not for his own sake, but for that of king and country. How he fulfilled this resolve is really the main story of this book.

The West Indies and Trouble

Nelson returned home to find that his uncle, at least, was getting on very well indeed, being now Comptroller of the Navy, but this hopeful fact was far outweighed by the dreadful knowledge that he himself would have to face his examination for a lieutenancy, an ordeal in which the victim, dressed in his best, and carrying with him the journals he had kept in all the ships in which he had served, along with progress reports from all his commanding officers, appeared before a board of captains who would fire broadsides of questions at him in a grimly inhuman manner. Nelson appeared, we are told, "somewhat alarmed," when he confronted his examiners, and, what was worst of all, in charge of the proceedings was his own uncle—gazing stonily at him as if he had never set eyes on him before.

However, once he started talking on subjects he knew and loved, Nelson's nerves left him, and he passed with distinction. Then, and only then, his uncle presented him to the other examiners as his nephew, and when they expressed their amazement that the Comptroller had given them no hint of the relationship, they received the reply that he had not wanted the "younker" to be favored. In any case, added Captain Suckling, he had known that the boy would do well.

The new lieutenant was now appointed to the *Lowestoffe* frigate, and sailed in her to the West Indies, where he made friends with a rather silent young lieutenant from the North Country—Cuthbert Collingwood. Nelson passed his examination for lieutenant on April 8, 1777, and on June 11, 1779, not yet twenty-one, he became a post captain, receiving command of the *Hinchinbrook*, 28 guns. However, it did not seem as if he would be enjoying his new authority for long; a great French fleet threatened Jamaica, and Nelson, offering his services for the defense of the island, gave his family the news that he might well become a prisoner of war by informing them that they must not be surprised to hear that he was beginning to learn French. Luckily the French commander never realized that Jamaica was completely at his mercy; the invasion never came, and the British authorities decided to swing over from the defensive and attack not France, but France's ally, Spain, and her great possessions in Central and South America.

Now how on earth did Nelson become involved in all this? His work was that of convoy—once he had landed the troops from Jamaica on that portion of the mainland ominously known as the Mosquito Coast, his job was over. But not a single man in the expeditionary force had ever been up the San Juan River; no one had the least idea where the enemy fortifications were; he could not let the unfortunate troops set off alone to blunder wildly about the South American continent. At least, he would carry them up the river as far as he could.

With two of his boats he began to go upriver. It was the end of the dry season, the worst time of the year, for the river was so low that the boats had to be dragged over sandbanks, and when water was deep enough to float in there were difficult currents and rapids. The soldiers, unaccustomed to fending for themselves, left everything to the resourceful sailors, but even the energy of Nelson's men began to wilt under the blazing sun, the glare of which was reflected from the white shoals. Evil green trees came down to the river, but brought no shade, only adding to the dreadful airlessness of the atmosphere, while at night there fell a heavy, unwholesome dew.

But nothing could quench Nelson's spirits when they came upon the first enemy outpost. It was he who led the attack, leaping ashore at the head of a handful of seamen with such vigor that he landed so heavily on the muddy bank that his shoes were stuck, so he rushed on barefoot, and, as he put it, boarded the battery. But though he did indeed bring the soldiers up to the chief enemy fortress, he did not see the end of the siege, being wholly engaged in fighting his own desperate battle against illness. He returned to Jamaica a living skeleton, having to be carrried ashore in his cot, while his ship's company had been practically wiped out—eighty-seven fell sick in a single night, and of a total of two hundred men, only ten survived.

Nelson's only hope of recovery lay in being sent home, so home he went, but remained in such a state of weakness that months passed before he was well enough to go to sea again. Now when the Admiralty dealt with a captain so recently desperately ill, still suffering from the effects of the West Indian climate, one might have expected such an officer to be sent—say to the Mediterranean. But the authorities did not think along these lines; he was sent off to spend the winter in the North Sea. He said obviously his superiors were trying to find out exactly how much punishment his health could stand.

He had a new ship—the 28-gun *Albermarle*, a perfectly hopeless vessel never intended for a warship at all, having started life as a French merchant vessel. She was an absolute brute to handle, and sailed badly; her new captain was convinced that the fact she was French-built was the root of the trouble; the enemy had taught her only to run away, and it was quite true that the only time she sailed well was running directly before the wind.

However, the months spent freezing in the North Sea had one beneficial result—though this lay in the distant future. Nelson gained firsthand knowledge of the Danish coast.

The *Albemarle*, however, continued to be an affliction; on more than one occasion she was nearly overturned because her masts were too long. No one could look forward to taking such a vessel across the Atlantic, but this is precisely what Nelson was ordered to do on his return from his Baltic cruise.

After proceeding to Canada, he was sent on a cruise to the south. He was supposed to go on convoy duty as far as New York, an assignment that would have made most men rub their hands in glee, for this was an excellent area for prize money. But it did not please the poor parson's son; he wanted to go further south, for if, as he remarked to the Admiral at New York, one might get rich quickly in these waters, the station for *honor* was the West Indies. So he went to the West Indies, came under the command of Lord Hood, whom he revered above all living admirals, and was introduced by Lord Hood to the King's son, Prince William, in words that showed Hood's own high opinion of the captain who had just joined his fleet—if the prince wished to ask any question regarding naval tactics, said the admiral, Captain Nelson could give him as much information as any officer in the fleet. The prince, for all his respect for the admiral's judgment, had his doubts at first, for Nelson, the merest boy of a captain, said his highness, was so oddly attired that the prince had "never seen anything like it before." But once the queer-looking creature began to talk, the prince was quite enchanted, and when he began to talk on naval matters, the prince realized he was listening to something quite out of the ordinary.

So began a friendship that was to endure—a very lucky thing for Nelson, one might think, to make friends with the King's son at the beginning of his career. But this friendship was to be the cause of despair and heartbreak.

Nelson had hoped that he might fight in a fleet engagement against the French, but soon after he arrived in the West Indies the war came to an end, the *Albemarle* returned to England, and Nelson, hearing that one might live more cheaply in France than in England, decided to kill two birds with one stone, and economize while at the same time learning the French language. So in the autumn of 1783 he went over to northern France, but the trip was anything but a success. He made little progress with the language, he found the country and its inhabitants dirty and inferior in all ways to his own, but what really spoiled the visit was the discovery that two brother officers—Captain Ball and Captain Shepherd—were actually imitating the horrid

French, because they had adopted the disgusting habit of wearing epaulettes. It was too bad, quite unforgivable— only the worst could be expected of such unpatriotic wretches.

So all he gained from his jaunt abroad was a detestation of Captain Ball; he was no further advanced with his French whatsoever. On his return to England, he was at once appointed to a 28-gun ship, the *Boreas,* going to the Leeward Islands, and taking as passengers the wife of the admiral on that station, Sir Richard Hughes, and his daughter, whom her mother was determined to marry off as soon as possible. Nelson, being a bachelor, could not help being uneasy. But if the admiral's wife and daughter gave him some bad moments on the voyage, the admiral himself gave him a far worse time at the end of it.

He was a one-eyed admiral, having lost the sight of one eye in an accident brought about by chasing a cockroach with a fork. Like Nelson himself, when it suited him he could turn a blind eye to what he did not choose to see, but, unlike Nelson in the next great war, when this admiral ignored anything, it was not for any heroic motive. The root of the trouble was this: at the end of the war just concluded, the Americans had gained their independence, but now they wanted both to have their cake and eat it—in other words, to be independent of Britain, but at the same time to enjoy the privileged trading position that had been theirs when they had been members of the empire.

The islanders were trading busily with the ex-rebels; Sir Richard Hughes saw it—and did nothing.

Luckily, Nelson's friend, Collingwood, was on the same station, and the two young officers called upon the admiral and asked him respectfully whether or not they were to guard their country's trade and see that its laws were obeyed —otherwise what was the point of Britain having a squadron on this station in times of peace? Sir Richard Hughes, inwardly raging at the insolence of these whipper-snappers, had to pretend to be convinced, and agreed that the acts should be enforced.

An admiral has many weapons with which he may injure a subordinate he dislikes. There were such things as reports to the Admiralty in which Captain Nelson might be described as a troublemaker, insubordinate—obedience is a magic word in the Navy—and while brother officers might back Nelson, their ships were scattered about the islands, and he had to fight his battles alone. Remember that he was a man who always craved affection, that he was young, just twenty-six, and, now that his Uncle was dead, was completely without influence and friends in high places. His admiral was his enemy, the rich merchants hated him, and were bent on his ruin. *They* had influence enough. It is difficult for us nowadays to realize how rich and important the West Indies were in Nelson's day, but then, when sugar was dear and slaves were cheap, the islands were the richest part of the empire, and a few years previously people in London had not minded losing the colonies on the American mainland, provided the all-important West Indies were safe. Among the merchants of the islands were millionaires; money has always talked with a loud voice, and in London the important West India Committee, which took care of the interests of these merchants, was listened to with deference by the government.

Meanwhile in the islands themselves Nelson was, at the best, an outcast, for none of the islanders save the Governor, Mr. Herbert, would speak to him.

Mr. Herbert's house was the only one Nelson might visit, but even there, surrounded by friends, it was difficult for him to relax. His host's niece described him as being "very silent" at dinner, drinking no wine until loyal toasts were given, with a "reserve and sternness in his behavior" that were entirely unlike the real Nelson. The lady went on to describe how she had done her best to get him to talk, but he would only say yes or no, and ended in despair that if only the cousin to whom she was writing had been there, *she* might have made something of him, "for you have been in the habit of attending to these odd sorts of people."

Eventually the young widowed lady to whom the letter was addressed did indeed meet "this strange man," but her small son had met him earlier, when the man "of whom everybody is so afraid," said Mr. Herbert, was discovered by the latter gentleman playing with little Josiah under the dining-room table, and not long afterward Nelson married the delicate Mrs. Nisbet. Nelson's wife has often been blamed by her husband's admirers because she could not understand his soaring enthusiasms and share his moods, but at least this should be said of her—that in the dark anxious days in the Leewards his affection for her must have given him some relief from the agony of apprehension that tormented him, while if she seemed unsympathetic in the days of his fame, when hundreds sought his friendship, she married him when he was universally shunned and detested.

Nelson's friend, Prince William, gave the bride away, and Nelson may have reflected that even if the admiral and governors and merchants hated him, he had little to fear, with the king's son his friend, while the government at home, of course, could not fail to approve the way in which he had put the interests of the country before all things. How wrong he was he found soon enough, when he returned to England in June, 1787, three months after his marriage.

Nelson was on half pay (8 shillings, or about 25¢, a day) from November 1787 to February 1793, and he saw action again only because the country faced such danger that even an officer who had offended so unforgivably might be given employment once more. What was his crime? His admiral said he was a troublemaker; American and West Indian merchants were determined on his ruin. There is one story that shows in a horribly clear light the kind of persecution he underwent.

He was very poor of course, and with his wife was living with his father in Norfolk. His greatest ambition now was to have a horse of his own, and since he could not pay much, he set out one day for a local fair, hoping to pick up a bargain. In his absence two men rudely forced their way into his father's home, and demanded to see him. Being disappointed in this, they demanded to see his wife. After they had made the poor frightened lady declare time and again that she was indeed his wife, they gave her a paper containing the information that the American traders were claiming damages of £20,000 (about $100,000) from Nelson.

Nelson, meanwhile, had bought his horse, and returned home in soaring spirits, calling to his wife to come and admire his bargain, holding forth on all its good points as if he were the greatest expert on horseflesh in the world instead of a rider no better than the sailor usually is. But then something in her manner made him uneasy; he checked his excited talk and asked her what was amiss; she told him. He, who had been like a small boy with a new toy, became very cold and grim. If the government did not support him, he must fly from England and take refuge in France. The alternative was a debtor's prison, with no hope of release. But at least the government refused to let *this* charge be pressed against him.

Yet what he wanted, of course, was leave to go to sea again—for that he was eating his heart out. England's relations with foreign powers reached danger point, she mobilized her fleets—surely she might find something for a man who had written to his wife a few months before their marriage, "our country has the first demand for our services," a man whom Lord Hood, greatest of living sea officers, had said was a brilliant tactician? To Lord Hood, indeed, Nelson applied for help in 1790, when England was on the brink of war with Spain, and Lord Hood, who admired him and was his friend, had now to tell him something that would break his heart. There was very little chance, Lord Hood said gravely, that he would ever be employed again; he did not understand the seriousness of the situation; the *King* was opposed to him.

He would never be employed again because of his friendship with the King's son, that son who had acted rashly, disobediently in the West Indies. Nelson, heaven only knows, had done his best in the way of restraint, but the King, always obstinate and prejudiced, now a little mad, thought otherwise. Nelson had been a bad influence, Nelson was a friend of his undutiful son. So he could look for no further employment.

He went back to Norfolk. His father noted that he was restless; his wife recalled later that at times he talked of entering the Russian service. Spring followed spring; he went shooting (though anything but an expert shot), and in search of birds' nests, and with the aid of the boy who cleaned the boots and knives he constructed a dam across the stream, for in the endless candlelit winter evenings he had made for himself a model ship of the line. Likely enough that was the only ship that would be his now—just as in those same long evenings, he would give up staring at his nautical charts, and fall to reading Dampier's *Voyages*, with the bitter thought that his own voyaging days were over, and he could travel now only through a printed page. And time passed slowly, terribly slowly.

Meanwhile, across the Channel a Revolution intended to bring peace and brotherhood brought bloodshed and the threat of war. England must fight a terrible foe, and her shield must be her fleet. She must use every ship, she must use every man—even a man previously doomed to unemployment because of royal disfavor. Surprisingly, the Admiralty suddenly decided that what really mattered was Captain Nelson's professional ability. He was offered the 64-gun *Agamemnon* and told by Lord Hood, hoisting his flag in the *Victory,* that he might be ordered to join his lordship's Mediterranean command. On February 7, 1793, Nelson took command of his first line of battleships, and his life began again.

But it had been a near thing. Too often we think of Nelson's naval career as if it covered only the twelve and a half years following his recall to active service; too rarely do we remember the five years of hopelessness and heartbreak because people of wealth and influence from the King down had tried to ruin, to destroy him. Do not let us forget, when thinking of Vice-admiral Viscount Nelson, conquerer of the Nile, the Baltic, and Trafalgar, that behind him stands half-pay, sick at heart Captain Nelson, sailing a toy ship, told he would never be employed again, thinking of joining the Russian Navy. The history of the world would have been changed had he done so!

Black Days in the Mediterranean

Nelson's first fighting was, oddly enough, not at sea; in fact, he turned soldier, and besieged French-held fortresses in Corsica.

When Nelson went to the Mediterranean in 1793, Malta still belonged to the Knights of St. John, and Lord Hood therefore seemed to be in luck's way when he was offered the island of Corsica by the freedom-loving islanders, who loathed French rule. However, he was to find, regrettably, that the main obstacle to his getting possession of Corsica was not so much the French garrisons but the British Army. Or, more accurately, its commanding officer, General Dundas.

There was no lack of British troops in Corsica, where their red coats clustered thick as clumps of scarlet poppies on the hills—but they did nothing. "Armies go so slow that seamen think they never mean to go forward," commented Captain Nelson, to whom Lord Hood entrusted the command of the seamen sent to besiege Bastia.

General Dundas had five regiments lying idle at St. Fiorenzo. He did not give Lord Hood the assistance of one.

The naval landing began on April 4, 1794. "Brigadier" Nelson—he had acquired this title from the army—lovingly watched the crew of the *Agamemnon* as they imperturbably hauled great guns up heights where military officers had said it was quite impossible to drag them even if teams of mules tugged at them. Aglow with admiration he watched them charge into action, and wrote, "My seamen are now what British seamen ought to be, almost invincible. They really mind shot no more than peas." They were few, he said happily, but of the right sort—and, sure enough, before the end of May, Bastia, with its much larger defending force, fell to the sailors.

The siege of Calvi, the second French-held Corsican fortress, was much the same as the siege of the first—unending toil for the sailors, with twenty-five heavy guns to be man-handled up precipitous heights, for, said Nelson, "We will fag ourselves to death before any blame shall lie at our doors." It was the time of year we call the dog days, and what the Corsicans themselves call the lion sun. Fever played havoc with the besiegers; over half of them were stricken, and the rest looked like so many ghosts. Nelson himself, for a wonder, escaped a bad bout; he himself explained it by saying that though all the various diseases attacked him, he had not enough strength for them to get their teeth into. Yet do not think him lucky; one hot sunny morning an enemy shot struck the ground near him, driving sand and gravel into one of his eyes and so destroying the sight. He reported to Lord Hood that he had been a little hurt, and absented himself from the siege for one day.

Yet he could show rage and despair enough if he chose, and proved as much in face of another misfortune. By this time the position of the British in the Mediterranean grew gloomier day by day—Italian allies deserted, and Spain was growing ominously cool. I think you will agree from what has gone before that Lord Hood was the last man to fear facing odds, but he believed that the Admiralty might very well spare him some reinforcements—no brave man hesitates to tackle great odds in a good cause, but at the same time no sensible man likes being outnumbered if he can help it. Yet letters home seemed to have no effect; the old admiral therefore decided to go to make the appeal in person.

The First Lord of the Admiralty was Lord Spencer. He was patriotic, able and hardworking, yet too conscious of the fact that he was *very* blueblooded. At the best he was always a little patronizing to sea officers. He had his own definite ideas as to how an admiral should approach the god that ruled his destinies—himself—and however Lord Hood asked for reinforcements, it was not in the way Lord Spencer felt it should be done. So Lord Hood, England's most famous sailor, was dismissed—in the interests of discipline—and never employed again in the service of his country.

But do not think that the men of the Mediterranean Fleet took their chief's dismissal lightly. Above all, do not think that Nelson, who had also been the heartbroken victim of dislike in high places, felt no grief, no rage. What he wrote is famous: "O, miserable Board of Admiralty. They have served the first officer in our service away from his command . . ."

41

But this was not all; the situation was bad enough because Lord Hood was not coming back, but it about reached rock bottom when appalled officers brooded on the character of the man taking his place. This was Admiral Hotham, an elderly gentleman of whom someone said unkindly, "his soul has got down to his belly and never mounts higher now." Poor Nelson found himself—not for the last time—under the command of an admiral "alarmed at the mention of any strong measure." A fleet action—the ships of the line of the British Mediterranean fleet engaging the ships of the Toulon fleet on one of the latter's rare trips to sea—might fairly accurately be described as a strong measure. It also goes without saying it was what the British had been praying for for months. This opportunity, for which the fiery Nelson might have given his other eye, was *twice* offered to Admiral Hotham—twice he was within striking distance of the enemy. But he dilly-dallied and twice lost the opportunity of forcing a battle—a general battle, that is, for Nelson and the *Agamemnon,* the smallest battleship in the fleet, fought a kind of private war against the Toulon squadron, hurling himself undaunted at a retreating enemy giant of eighty guns like a tiger leaping at the throat of a water-buffalo, clawing it to a standstill, mauling it, and showing every readiness to take on the entire enemy squadron single-handed—for his admiral was content to watch him through his spyglass. When Nelson, master of two prizes, begged him to chase the flying foe, Hotham replied blandly, "We must be contented; we have done very well."

Nelson made three comments on this:

"Now had we taken ten sail, and allowed the eleventh to escape, when it had been possible to have got at her, I could never have called it well done."

"To say how much we wanted Lord Hood at that time is to say, will you have all the French Fleet or no action."

"I wish to be an admiral, and in the command of the English Fleet; I should very soon do much, or be ruined; my disposition cannot bear tame and slow measures. Sure I am, had I commanded on the 14th, that either the whole French Fleet would have graced my triumph, or I should have been in a confounded scrape."

In this last comment is a prophecy of all that was to occur before Aboukir and Trafalgar.

But Aboukir and Trafalgar still lie in the future, and Captain Nelson is still chafing under the command of Admiral Hotham, still disturbing that easygoing gentleman by appearing aboard the flagship from time to time and suggesting various "strong" measures. If the French Fleet were comfortably out of sight, the restless fellow is making mad suggestions about making life unpleasant for a French army on land. There is, for example, this upstart young General Bonaparte, about to descend on the rich, helpless cities of Italy with an army supposedly out to liberate, but really out to loot. Nelson becomes absurdly excited over this; badgers his admiral with ideas of attacking the enemy lines of communication along the Riviera coast . . .

But at this point the admiral who was a man of straw gave place to the admiral his own king called "Old Oak."

Sir John Jervis was a grim man. As a boy he had known poverty, and humiliation because of that poverty, and so he had taken on a kind of stern armor. The general opinion was that though he was an excellent seaman, as a man he was as harsh and austere as any Spartan, that where discipline was concerned he was a little mad, and as for a little human sympathy, Sir John Jervis had never heard of that quality.

Now try to picture Nelson under the command of such

an admiral—oversensitive Nelson, who craved for affection and trust and sympathy. What did Nelson say on the subject?

He wrote to the ogre himself. "We look up to you, as we have always found you, as to our Father, under whose fostering care we have been led to fame."

As for Jervis' attitude to Nelson, the great victory won by the younger sailor off the mouth of the Nile could never have happened if Jervis had not selected Nelson for the task, protected him against the violent criticisms of other admirals and members of the government, and gone on trusting him during long months of waiting when a sick old admiral scotched mutiny like a snake, knowing that he had given the best of his ships to a subordinate who must have missed the French—which meant that at any moment he, with the great weapon he had forged and tempered given to another, might with an inferior force be called upon to fight the Toulon Fleet bearing Bonaparte and a great army to the conquest of Ireland.

Now how did such extraordinary trust and confidence spring up between two characters who seemed so dissimilar? Make no mistake about it—Nelson might be brilliant, but at the same time he was a subordinate most admirals would prefer to do without. You will find that most brilliant commanders proved, in their earlier days, most difficult subordinates, and as far as, say Admirals Hughes and Hotham had been concerned, Nelson had been quite unendurable, because every time he had opposed them he had been *right*. That, of course, was quite unforgivable. Now Admiral Jervis, of course, was the last man to turn a blind eye to lawbreaking, like Hughes, or to be lackadaisical, like Hotham, *but* he worshipped discipline, and Nelson had a reputation for insubordination. Therefore, when Nelson sailed to meet the new commander-in-chief, his friends might well be fearful, and his enemies excited.

Nelson himself must have thought along these lines as he was rowed across to the flagship, the *Victory*, in Fiorenzo Bay. He knew that Sir John was "a man of business"—a joyful change after Admiral Hotham. At the same time he had prophesied that the change in command would cause "great joy to some, and sorrow to others." The point was, in which ranks would Nelson find himself?

Picture him pondering on this as the boat skims over the water, as he boards the flagship to the wail and twitter of the boatswain's pipe, as he is ushered below to the great cabin where his fate awaits him. He must have known that this was the decisive moment of his career—all depended on Sir John's attitude towards him.

So they faced each other, and Sir John stared at the captain's untidy clothes—yet looked longer at the captain's eyes and mouth. No doubt he had heard that Nelson could be wildly temperamental as any prima donna—yet in any crisis, by all accounts, he turned cold and grim. Sir John knew something of this type of officer. Yes, Sir John knew this type, all nerves beforehand; steady as a rock, ice cool in the swirl and heat of battle. And he recognized brains and resolution; in methods he and Nelson were never alike— "Where I would take a penknife Lord St. Vincent takes a hatchet," Nelson remarked on one occasion—but they realized that each man knew his weapon best, and there in the admiral's cabin of the *Victory* began the great alliance that was to lead to some of the greatest deeds in all the long history of the Royal Navy.

On December 2, 1796, one of the blackest days in the history of the Royal Navy, the Mediterranean Fleet anchored off Gibraltar—one of the blackest days because, for the first

45

time for generations, not a single British ship lay or cruised on the waters of the great inland sea.

Why had the fleet left the Mediterranean? Because no fleet can keep control of any stretch of water without bases, and bases were precisely what Britain lacked in these sad winter months. The numerous Italian states that had been allies closed their ports to British ships, for they dreaded the French army storming across Italy, while Spain, jealous because of British action in Corsica and in the West Indies, had swung right over from friend to foe. Spain had a big fleet, but her chief weapon as far as Britain in the Mediterranean was concerned, was geography—Spanish geography, one way or another, has always been a tough nut for her enemies to crack.

Not that the men of the Mediterranean Fleet ever thought there was the slightest reason to evacuate the Mediterranean —the order came from the home government, and Nelson, for one, was demanding, "Do his Majesty's ministers know their own minds?" "They at home," he went on to say, "do not know what this fleet is capable of performing—anything and everything."

"Orders in sackcloth and ashes!" he exploded.

He might argue here, "What about Corsica? Surely we were not going to let *that* go?"

They were. Nelson was entrusted with the responsible and tricky task of seeing that the British forts in Corsica were dismantled, and removing the guns and stores, difficult enough in any case since heavy rains had broken up such roads as Corsica possessed, while in addition a French force had already landed in the island. However, as Sir John wrote proudly, "trouble was a word which had long ceased to be found in a sailor's dictionary."

After the evacuation Nelson received his first promotion since the beginning of the war—he was made commodore.

Corsica had gone; now Elba must go—and since Nelson had managed the evacuation of Corsica so well, he was sent to supervise the evacuation of the smaller island. He hoisted his broad pennant—proud sign of his new rank—in a frigate, the *Minerve,* and proceeded on his mission in company with another small vessel, only to fall in with Britain's new enemy in the shape of a Spanish frigate. For three hours the *Minerve* fought the enemy vessel which only gave up after she had lost 164 men and all her officers save one, her captain.

Another enemy frigate appeared on the horizon, and shortly afterward engaged the *Minerve,* and when after a combat of half an hour, the new enemy had received such a hammering from the dauntless *Minerve* that she beat a retreat, an entire enemy squadron—two frigates and two ships of the line came into sight. However, their chief anxiety seemed to be that the captured ship should be recovered, and by relinquishing his prey, Nelson was able to escape. Abandoning the captured vessel meant, of course, abandoning the prize crew he had set aboard her, which he loathed doing, and as soon as he reached Elba, he wrote to the governor of the nearest Spanish port, arranging an exchange of prisoners. One of the latter was a gigantic lieutenant with a soft Dorset accent—Lieutenant Thomas Hardy.

Nelson rushed through the evacuation of Elba at lightning speed; he wanted to carry out not only his orders, but a program he had mapped out for himself, which included having a look at the enemy at Toulon and Cartagena in order to be able to take back up-to-date news of them.

But at Cartagena there *was* no enemy fleet—the Spanish dons were out. There was news of them at the Rock—they had passed westward, and Sir John Jervis, resolved that they should never link up with the French fleets based to the north, had taken up his battle station off Cadiz. Nelson sped

47

to join him, halting only to take on board the returned British prisoners.

It was not long before the latter must have started to think that their freedom was going to prove a very brief thing indeed, for two Spanish ships of the line and a frigate began to chase the *Minerve*. A passenger, watching the *Minerve* clearing for action, asked Nelson if he thought it would come to a fight. "Very possibly," replied Nelson, and added, staring grimly up at his pennant, "before the Dons get hold of that bit of bunting, I will have a struggle with them, and sooner than give up the frigate, I'll run her ashore."

The short February day was drawing to a close; dusk was beginning to fall, but it did not seem as if night would save them, for the enemy was fast overhauling them. However, down they all trooped at the usual time for dinner—men always fight best on a full stomach, and Lieutenant Hardy for one, being so recently out of a Spanish prison, was determined to have a decent English meal inside him before facing the horrors of don cooking again.

As he chewed meditatively, and replied politely to the congratulations of his neighbor on his escape, his trained sailor's ear was strained to catch all the familiar sounds of preparation for action, for the cry of the lookout, but when a call did come, it was totally unexpected—and the most unwelcome in the world.

"Man overboard!"

That some lubberly member of the crew should choose *this*, of all moments, to fall over the side! Still, Lieutenant Hardy knew his duty—he pounded up on deck, supervised the lowering of the jolly boat, got inside it, and began to search for the missing man, first the white wake of the ship, then the dark, menacing waters astern—more and more astern, for the current was running strongly eastward, that is, it was carrying Hardy and the crew of the jolly boat further and further away from the *Minerve,* and more and more into the jaws of the enemy.

Lieutenant Hardy saw the gates of the prison house looming close, but he doggedly went on with his task, until it was quite clear that there was no hope. Then he signalled, "No sign of the missing man," and gave his crew the order to regain the frigate—if they could.

They pulled and sweated in that cold gloom for dear life, but the current fought them, the enemy gathered round for the kill. Lieutenant Hardy, with one swift, considering glance, saw that by this time the enemy were within gunshot of the *Minerve* herself. Ah, well, the jolly boat might yet play her part, for if the enemy stopped to take her, it might give the Commodore a chance to slip away.

But the Commodore, as it suddenly appeared to Hardy's straining, incredulous eyes, had other ideas. *Minerve,* instead of running for her life, was backing her mizzen-topsail, dropping down towards the tiny fugitive. She was deliberately coming within range of the enemy guns, and Hardy, in a kind of agony, thought her destruction was a matter of minutes now.

But the Spanish pursuers, chivalrous to a fault though they themselves might be, could not understand the madness of the Englishman. No officer would cold-bloodedly hazard himself and his ship for the sake of a lieutenant and crew of a jolly boat, *that* was not the reason he was offering action —no, obviously he had sighted his main fleet steering in from the west, and the Spaniards were not going to allow themselves to fall for so transparent a trick. So they, too, shortened sail, the jolly boat was picked up, and as darkness fell Hardy found himself back on the familiar deck he had never thought to see again.

He was never very good at putting his feelings in words, so very likely he said very little to the Commodore, but we can imagine his reaction when he heard how the Commodore had exclaimed, "By God! I'll not lose Hardy!" He would remember all this as long as he lived—we cannot doubt that it returned to his mind some eight and half years after, in more or less the same spot, at the entry to the Straits, not far from Cadiz, off the Cape called Trafalgar.

Commodore Nelson, therefore, when he rejoined Sir John Jervis on the eve of February 14, had a most acceptable valentine to present to his commander-in-chief. The dons were out—Nelson had, in fact, sailed through their main fleet during the night following Hardy's rescue, and had informed his passengers that if the great ships surrounding them were sailing across the Atlantic, why, then he too was West Indies bound in order that the commanders there might receive warning. However, the Spanish had nothing so enterprising in mind, and meant to proceed to Cadiz, and when in the morning of the thirteenth Nelson saw them haul up on a course for that great port, he himself had crammed on every stitch of canvas, and had hastened westward with the news.

Even now, of course, Sir John's anxieties were not over— if the dons could waddle into Cadiz before he could get at them, he would be confronted not with the prospect of a battle but the infinitely more dreary future of an interminable and tedious blockade. He did not go to bed that night.

But for once the wind favored him—a gale blew from the east, and drove the helpless dons past Cadiz and ever closer to the waiting British fleet. By this time they were in considerable disorder, and throughout the night they were firing signal guns, which was helpful to the British but of singularly little benefit to themselves. By dawn they were straggling all over the sea, while Sir John's own vessels were revealed in the first grey light as still being in the close order enjoined upon them the night before—indeed, in such close formation had the ships sailed that captain had been able to talk with captain from respective quarter-decks. So perfect was the order kept in his fleet that even Sir John was surprised into expressing high approval of his captains.

And then he said, almost to himself, "A victory is very essential to England at this moment."

Visibility was poor, and the mist was slow in clearing. It was only by degrees that Sir John became aware of the odds against him.

"There are eight sail of the line, Sir John."

"Very well, sir."

"There are twenty sail of the line, Sir John."

"Very well, sir."

"There are twenty-five sail of the line, Sir John."

"Very well, sir."

"There are twenty-seven sail of the line, Sir John."

"Enough, sir, no more of that," exclaimed the admiral; "the die is cast; and if there are fifty sail, I will go through them."

There was a slightly different atmosphere in the Spanish fleet. According to one account, the admiral believed that Jervis had no more than nine ships in his fleet—whether this were true or no, he, like Jervis, could have no idea as to the real numbers he would have to face until the fog cleared. Then the Spanish lookout ship further complicated matters. Her captain, exasperated because he felt his signals were being disregarded, made a fresh signal—that the enemy had forty ships of the line. He said later that he did this to give his admiral a good shaking up, but, of course, such a terrifying message would have anything but a rousing effect on such a person as the Spanish commander-in-chief who, with the greater part of his fleet, fell into a horrible state of alarm and despondency—there was no "If there are fifty sail, I will go through them," from Don Joseph de Cordova.

Nelson Insures a Victory

And Nelson? He was back in a ship of the line again. He had hoisted his flag in the *Captain*, commanded by Captain Ralph Willett Miller.

The battle began at eleven-thirty, at which time the *Culloden*, commanded by Troubridge, who led the British column, opened fire on one of the two straggling divisions, widely separated, of the enemy fleet. Jervis' ships were in one long line, sterns and bowsprits almost touching—the *Captain* sailed third from the rear.

At noon Troubridge actually broke the enemy line, and an hour later came the climax of the battle. The British, coming down on the Spaniards from the north, had broken the line of one of the enemy divisions (the windward division) but the leeward division of nine ships was still some miles away, untouched, while the eighteen ships of the windward division, though badly mauled, still had two chances of escape. One by one the British vessels that had broken the line must turn towards the north in order to re-engage the enemy, but that would take time—and the Spanish admiral might use that time either to make for Cadiz (for the wind had changed) or to effect a linkup with the untouched division of nine ships—in which case, when the British *did* renew the action, they would have twenty-seven vessels to contend with. Already the Spanish windward division was beginning to alter course to join up with the leeward division.

Then Nelson, third from the rear of the English line, saw what the enemy intended—saw also, we are often told, his great blazing chance of glory. If a vision of golden triumph danced before his eyes, so did something in plain black and white—Instruction Sixteen of the *Fighting Instructions*, the Ten Commandments of the naval officer. And Instruction Sixteen ran as follows:

"In all cases of fight with the enemy, the commanders of His Majesty's ships are to keep the fleet *in one line*, and (as much as may be) to preserve that order of battle, which they have been directed to keep before the time of fight."

Never think that Nelson was unaware of these instructions —and the possible penalty of transgressing them. But at the same time he was even more aware that Jervis' main fleet would never be able to tack and overhaul the retreating enemy—that the two Spanish divisions might link up or scurry into Cadiz unless . . .

(Picture his racing brain estimating chances!)

. . . unless they were prevented from doing so by a captain from the rear of the British line who ran his ship athwart the bows of the ships in the center of the Spanish windward division. Stopped them. Made them fight.

That captain would be more or less committing suicide by so doing . . . to engage say half a dozen Spanish monsters with one of the smallest warships present. But he would stop the enemy escape gap, would give his comrades time to come up and complete the hammering from which the dons were fleeing.

Nelson told Miller to bear out of line and steer straight for the center of the enemy. He might have reflected at this moment that if he escaped being blown out of the water, he would still have to face a charge of flouting the *Fighting Instructions*, disobeying his admirals' signal.

With the 74-gun *Captain* he engaged the *Santissima Trinidad*, 136 guns, the largest warship afloat, the *San Joseph*, 112 guns, the *Salvador del Mundo*, 112 guns, the *San Nicolas*, 80 guns, the *San Isidro*, 74 guns, another 74, and yet another.

Miraculously the *Captain* was not blown out of the water in the first five minutes; miraculously she took that almost unimaginable pounding for almost an hour, by which time Troubridge in the *Culloden* and Collingwood in the *Excellent* were supporting Nelson, and the rest of the fleet was coming up—and the dons had not been able to get away.

By this time Nelson had done more than enough to ensure victory for his country—he might limp with all honor out of the fight. Indeed, the *Captain* was good for nothing now —she could not fight, she could not maneuver, she could not chase. Her fore-topmast was gone, her wheel was shot away, not a stitch of sail, not a shred of shroud or rope was left to her. The wonder was that she was still afloat.

But Nelson was happiest in the hottest fire. The *Captain* was no good for fighting? He would find a use for her yet! As a matter of fact, he used her as a springboard—a springboard from which he might capture a Spanish giant or two. With roaring volunteers waving cutlasses behind him he sprang up into the mizzen-chains of the *San Nicolas*. A marine smashed in the window of the upper quarter-gallery, using his musket, and Nelson, followed by a party of boarders including three midshipmen, jumped in. They forced the cabin doors, drove back the Spanish officers who fired at them with pistols, pressed on to the quarter-deck, the forecastle, received the swords of surrendering Spanish officers, saw the proud Spanish flag hauled down—and received a burst of fire from the stern gallery of the even bigger Spanish giant ranged alongside the *San Nicholas*—the *San Joseph*. You may imagine the effect this had on the little group that had dared all, endured all. With a shout of "Westminster Abbey or victory!" Nelson stormed up the main-chains, wildly cheering seamen at his heels—at which a Spanish officer spoke hastily and wisely from the quarter-deck. "We surrender," he said.

So there stood Nelson, on the quarter-deck of his second prize, officers giving up their swords to him, and the *Victory* sailing past and cheering—the whole fleet were cheering like madmen.

But what did Sir John Jervis think, and what would he say?

That thought came like a dash of cold water.

Nelson, when the fighting died away, did not board the *Victory* in anything like the fearless mood in which he had stormed the enemy monsters.

There stood Sir John, formidable on his quarter-deck. There stood groups of officers, mostly with commiseration on their faces.

Sir John advanced on the apprehensive Nelson, took him in his arms, and hugged him. "My dear Nelson," he said, "I can never sufficiently thank you!"

Sir John was a great man.

But a petty-minded man could not leave well alone. Captain Calder that evening said that Nelson's maneuver "was an unauthorized departure from the prescribed mode of attack."

Everyone fell silent then, waiting to see how the old admiral would deal with the suggestion. He dealt with it in a masterly manner. "It certainly was," he said, shooting a keen look at Calder from beneath shaggy brows, "and if ever you commit such a breach of your orders I will forgive *you*."

Sir John became an earl, and took his title from the victory he had won. Nelson was knighted. He also received promotion, became rear admiral of the Blue. Already the Nelson legend was beginning—all the fleet talked about "Nelson's patent bridge for boarding first-rates." In England balladsingers in the street were singing of him. It was a dark year for England, faithless allies falling away abroad, rebellion at home, invasion ever-threatening, but in that threatening sky a light had appeared in the west, from the surges of the sea, and those who saw that light on the far horizon might hope and take heart once more.

Now Rear Admiral Nelson shifted his flag to a new ship— a bigger, but not a better ship, for the *Theseus* had lately taken part in the mutiny that had left the Spithead Fleet paralyzed. Her crew was unchanged and it was feared that their ideas too had not altered. The *Theseus* was, indeed, as Lord St. Vincent put it grimly, "an abomination"; however, the old admiral hoped that if Nelson and Miller went to her they *might* work a miracle. And indeed they did; only a few weeks after the change in command a paper, signed in the name of the ship's company, was dropped on the quarter-deck. It ran as follows:

"Success attend Admiral Nelson! God bless Captain Miller! We thank them for the officers they have placed over us. We are happy and comfortable, and will shed every drop of blood in our veins to support them, and the name of the *Theseus* shall be immortalized as high as the *Captain's*."

No officer could have a finer tribute—but unfortunately the fervent wish of the seamen did not come true. They saw action with Nelson, but it was in sad contrast to the glory and thrilling excitement of Cape St. Vincent. He took the *Theseus* on the expedition to Teneriffe.

If you ever read a guide to Santa Cruz de Teneriffe, you will find that one of the principal holidays is July 25, the anniversary of the repulse of the attack led by Nelson in 1797. In the museum you will see carefully preserved the actual gun (El Tigre) which gave Nelson his wound, and in a dark corner of the cathedral is a tattered British flag. But where is Teneriffe, and why did Nelson go there?

Teneriffe is the capital of the Canary Islands—peaks of a volcanic mass thrusting up into the South Atlantic, far closer to Africa than to Europe. To these islands Spanish conquerors had gone three hundred years before, and in these islands more recently, in the months following the battle of Cape St. Vincent, the British believed the Spanish Viceroy of Mexico, homeward bound for Cadiz, had taken refuge. But the Viceroy was not the magnet drawing Nelson to the distant islands—the magnet was the treasure (supposedly between six and seven million pounds) that he was carrying back with him to Spain. Spain was completely dependent on the safe arrival of the annual treasure fleet from the Americas. Capture that treasure fleet and you knocked Spain out of the war.

No doubt another admiral silently influenced Nelson, though his mighty heart had stopped beating nearly a century and a half before—Robert Blake, who on April 14, 1657, had gone into Teneriffe and had captured six galleons crammed with silver. But Blake had been helped by the wind. You will find that Horatio Nelson never had that luck.

Do you think, though, that he was unaware of the tremendous importance of the wind in this expedition above all? "I do not reckon myself equal to Blake," he wrote to his commander-in-chief, "but if I recollect right, he was more obliged to the wind coming off the land, than to any exertions of his own . . ." In fact, in order to have more hope of success Nelson asked for a small force of troops; St. Vincent did all he could but not a man was forthcoming. It would have to be an entirely naval expedition, then—but had they not managed handsomely in Corsica? At any rate, when it departed on July 14, it sailed, said Lord St. Vincent, "upon a well-grounded hope of success." Certainly he had done all he could for Nelson, who had been allowed to choose the ships and men to accompany him—three ships of the line (*Theseus, Culloden, Zealous*), three frigates (*Seahorse, Terpischore, Emerald*), and Captains Miller, Troubridge, and Hood (a relation of Lord Hood), Fremantle, Bowen, Waller—and there was genuine affection in his parting message:

"God bless and preserve you . . . . you will deserve success; to mortals is not given the power of commanding it."

Disaster and Futile Search

There were two attacks on Teneriffe, on the 21st and the
24th of July. In the first attack the wind failed and Troubridge, of all men, wasted three hours in coming back to
ask what he was to do next. It was strange, this indecision
on the part of the man who had led the line at St. Vincent,
and who, as Commander of the forces to be landed at
Teneriffe, was given full scope to use his initiative. Note
that Nelson himself did not take part in the first attack—
the frigates went in with the landing parties, and Nelson

61

himself sailed eastward with the three 74s, to spend a long night waiting, waiting, waiting, straining eyes for distant gunflashes, straining ears for the sound of shots and a distant British cheer. Just before dawn he could bear it no longer; he took his squadron in towards Teneriffe to meet a crestfallen party returning—wind and current had been unfavorable, reported Troubridge, so it had been impossible to carry out the original plan. However, he believed it would be quite possible to storm from the rear the fort that had been the objective.

True, it *might* have been possible at midnight when, though the vessels had been seen, so total surprise was out of the question, the astonished enemy were still in a state of utter confusion, but by the time Troubridge reported to Nelson, it was six o'clock, and by the time a fresh attack could be made it was nine—broad daylight, with the enemy fully roused now, and fully prepared. All chance of success was gone. Without troops, all hope had lain in surprise— Troubridge must have known this, must have known, once the initial attack failed, that speed was everything, and yet, although Nelson had given him practically a free hand in what to do and how to do it, he felt he must go back to ask for fresh instructions, and, by so doing, threw the last chance away.

What was Nelson to do? He decided to try to get the landing parties ashore in broad daylight, with the ships of the line making a diversion in their favor by bombarding the fortress. But the wind—the wrong wind, or lack of wind —killed this hope too, for such a calm fell that the big ships could not get within range, and when a breeze finally arose it developed into a gale that kept the squadron offshore for another two days.

Nelson had always known that everything would depend on favorable winds and tides, and, these being against him, no one could blame him for giving up the attempt. But he could not bear to abandon hope, to return to his admiral to report a tame failure—on the morning of the 24th he decided to make a direct attack on the town itself, and he would lead this attack himself. He knew what a desperate thing this was, and this was probably the reason he chose to lead the attack in person; but also, of course, the recent bitter experience no doubt played its part in making him decide *not* to leave the carrying out of. his plans to others. So by five-thirty that evening the squadron was anchored two miles off the town. Josiah Nisbet, Nelson's stepson, received reluctant permission to be one of the landing party, and Nelson himself, after sorting and burning his wife's letters (he himself, in company with those who were taking part in the landing, did not really hope for success), was penning his last dispatch to St. Vincent, recommending his stepson "should I fall," to both the old admiral and to the Duke of Clarence. This was at eight o'clock. At half-past ten the members of the landing party began to go aboard the boats tossing alongside the frigates; by eleven the last boat was on its way.

The plan of attack—a rash, foolish attack, but to Nelson it was a point of honor—was simple. The assailants were to land on the breakwater, then make their way with all possible speed to the great square in the center of the town, after which they would act as events demanded.

It was a long pull to the shore, two and half hours' rowing in vile, blustery weather in intense darkness—not that they minded the darkness, of course, for it gave them cover, and a slight hope that after all they might land unperceived. But as they drew close the blackness was suddenly illuminated with blue flares, church bells clanged a warning, and a hail of shot—thirty to forty pieces of cannon as well as lines of muskets—lashed the oncoming boats. Still they went on, through the hail and the raging surf, to the breakwater.

Nelson was hit in the right elbow by grapeshot as he was drawing his sword, and as he fell, he transferred the weapon to his left hand, resolving not to leave it behind. His stepson, Josiah, just behind him, caught him and carried him back to the boat, placing him at the bottom, and covering with his hat the shattered arm, lest the sight of the great gush of blood should make his stepfather faint. With silk hand-kerchiefs from his own neck he made a tourniquet—without which Nelson assuredly would have died—while one of the bargemen, named Lovel, tore up his shirt, to make a sling. But these, of course, were only temporary measures; if Nelson were to have any chance of survival he must be got back to the ship—and how, we may imagine Josiah asking himself in despair, was this to be done, with the boat aground and the gauntlet of the terrible enemy fire to be run even if they got the boat afloat again?

Yet they did it—somehow. He and Lovel got hold of five other seamen, and after prodigious efforts, the boat was floated again. Josiah himself took one of the oars, and with sudden inspiration ordered the steersman to go close under the guns of the enemy battery, for in that way there was a slender chance of eluding its fire. The sound of the strained young voice roused Nelson, who said faintly that he wished to be lifted up, to look about him. Josiah did as he was asked, and so the wounded man looked about him at the orange gun-flashes spearing the darkness, at the eerie blue of flares lighting a stormy sea—and then there came a dreadful cry from the *Fox* cutter, hit below the waterline, holed, and sunk in a single nightmare moment. Of her 180 men, only 83 were saved, mostly by Nelson himself. He knew very well he might be bleeding to death, the pain of his wound was indescribable, yet he deliberately doubled risk and racking pain in order to save lives. And even when, reluctantly, he agreed there were no other poor comrades he might help, and the oarsmen bent to their toil again, and soon the side of a ship loomed up high above them, he refused to go aboard her, though Josiah in grief and terror warned him that any delay might cost him his life. His reason? The ship was the *Seahorse;* aboard her was Captain Fremantle's young wife; Fremantle himself was heaven knew where in the fiery inferno of Teneriffe. So:

"I had rather suffer death than alarm Mrs. Fremantle, by letting her see me in this state when I can give her no tidings whatever of her husband."

But at last they came alongside the *Theseus.* Nelson refused all offers of assistance in boarding her—that would take time, and the boat was needed again inshore. He asked for nothing more than a single rope thrown over the side; this he twisted round his left hand, and went up saying that the surgeon must make haste, for he knew he must lose his right arm.

He knew what that wound might mean. In his own words, "A left-handed admiral will never again be considered as useful." To Lord St. Vincent, announcing his defeat, he wrote with infinitely painful toil that he had become a burden to his friends, and useless to his country. St. Vincent replied, "Mortals cannot command success; you and your companions have certainly deserved it, by the greatest degree of heroism and perseverance that ever was exhibited."

But all the old admiral's kindness could not prevent Nelson

from knowing that in all probability his days of service were over. He had resolved to take part in the attack on the sleeping town fully convinced that he would not come back, but while it had been fairly easy to reconcile himself to death, crippled unemployment for the rest of his life was an infinitely blacker prospect. It was this thought, rather than his wound, that tormented him throughout the journey home, the stay at Bath with his family, and the return to London that autumn night in 1797, when the news that Admiral Duncan had beaten the Dutch reached London.

Nowadays we cannot realize how ugly and dangerous a thing was the London mob, but in 1797 it was terrifying to the bravest of men. In those days a sign of rejoicing was illuminated windows, and on this particular night the mob roamed about full of bloodthirsty threats of what they would do to the "traitors" who kept their windows dark. But of course if a sick man is trying desperately to sleep, his room will be darkened to help him, there were no lights in the windows of Nelson's lodgings, and soon the mob was thundering at the door. Yet by this time his fame was so great that when the gang of roughs and rowdies learned who lived in that house, and why there were no candles in the windows, the leader said gruffly, "You shall hear no more from us tonight," and the whole crowd moved quietly away.

Then the miracle happened: against all hope, he recovered from his wound, and might look forward to active service again. At the end of November he enjoyed a night of sound sleep—the first he had known since July. His arm was suddenly almost free from pain. Now it began to mend fast, so fast that on December 8 he was sending to the clergyman at St. George's, Hanover Square, the church where his family always worshipped when in London, the following form of thanksgiving: "An officer desires to return thanks to Almighty God for his perfect recovery from a severe wound, and also for the many mercies bestowed on him."

On December 21 his appointment to the *Vanguard* was published; in the New Year he was to rejoin Lord St. Vincent. But before accompanying him back to the Mediterranean it is very instructive to look over his shoulder, as it were, and read the catalog of his past services which, as a matter of routine, he had to draw up before receiving his pension. The list ran as follows:

Four actions with enemy fleets

Three actions with boats

Four months' service on shore with the army

Command of the batteries at the sieges of Bastia and Calvi

The capture of seven sail of the line, six frigates, four corvettes, eleven privateers

The capture of nearly fifty merchant vessels

More than one hundred and twenty engagements with the enemy . . .

In all this service he had also, of course, lost an eye and an arm.

An imposing list indeed, glory enough and to spare for one man.

For one *ordinary* man.

But not enough for Nelson. The days of his true glory were only beginning and, as he was no common man, so this was to be no common glory.

"I am very happy to send you Sir Horatio Nelson again," wrote the First Lord of the Admiralty to Lord St. Vincent, "not only because I believe I cannot send you a more zealous, active, and approved officer, but because I have reason to believe that his being under your command will be agreeable to your wishes."

He did not have to wait long for the old earl's reactions. "I do assure your lordship that the arrival of Admiral Nelson has given me new life."

He soon found employment for him. The government knew that the enemy was making tremendous preparations in Toulon; therefore, two days after Nelson rejoined the Mediterranean Fleet, St. Vincent sent him off in the *Vanguard*, with two other ships of the line, *Orion* and *Alexander*, and a few frigates, to reconnoiter Toulon, only to receive, a little more than a fortnight later, orders from home informing him of something like a somersault in foreign policy.

What exactly was the new policy to be?

In the first place, it was risky—decidedly risky. The fate of Europe, wrote the First Lord—and he did not speak lightly—might at any moment depend on the appearance of a British squadron in the Mediterranean, for Austria, fearing French aggression in Italy, was considering recommencing the fight. Austria thought the great expedition preparing at Toulon had Naples as its objective; Britain was inclined to think the French would make rather for Ireland or Portugal; but, no matter what its destination, that fleet must be sought out and destroyed.

Risky indeed, but the kind of orders St. Vincent, or any naval officer worth his salt, *wanted* to receive.

Risky, and the fate of Europe depended upon it—and without hesitation the old admiral knew to whom he would entrust the all-important task. Nelson, and Nelson alone.

Since risks are being discussed, think for a moment what a tremendous risk St. Vincent was taking in making this choice. What did most people know about Nelson? That he soared into the limelight in the action with the Spanish fleet, yes, but also, and this more recently, that in another encounter with Spaniards he had failed disastrously. He was brave, admittedly, but was being brave enough? Was he not really *too* brave, a rash, foolhardy creature like Shakespeare's Harry Hotspur, thinking,

"It were an easy leap,

To pluck bright honor from the pale-faced moon"?

All well and good, perhaps, in a fierce border chieftain of the barbarous Middle Ages, but hardly the ideas proper to be entertained by a naval officer in the year of grace, 1798. Nelson was altogether too erratic, too highly colored an individual for most senior officers—useful as the commander of a single vessel, perhaps, where insane bravery did not come amiss, but never fit to hold an independent command, being entirely lacking in coolness, calculation, and common sense.

Also, of course, it should never be forgotten that the senior officers who protested so loudly against Nelson's appointment did not protest from purely unselfish motives. *They* wanted that command for themselves. Not a pleasant thought for Nelson, knowing how bitterly his appointment was attacked, knowing there were angry, jealous persons in places of influence hoping he would meet with another disaster, as at Teneriffe.

And not pleasant for St. Vincent, knowing that unless Nelson justified his choice—and nothing but a tremendous victory would be enough for this—his enemies would turn on him, and rend him.

Risks? St. Vincent faced risks enough—risk in his choice of a commander, risk in the fact that he must divide his fleet, knowing that Nelson might miss the French, who might very well sail west, in which case he himself would have to fight them with only half his force. What was his reaction to this? He sent Nelson ten ships, and those ships were the cream of his fleet. Such gallant generosity warms the heart and uplifts the spirit.

So off sped the fighting giants. . . . *Theseus* 74 (Captain Miller), *Culloden* 74 (Captain Troubridge), *Zealous* 74 (Captain Hood), *Swiftsure* 74 (Captain Hallowell) . . . the elegant Captain Foley in the *Goliath* (Foley spends a great deal of money in maintaining an up-to-date library, which Nelson is to bless in the future), Darby, a jovial Irishman in the vessel that the Admiralty called the *Bellerophon* and her crew the "Bully Ruffian," Westcott, who had risen from the lower deck to command the *Majestic,* and Louis in the *Minotaur,* Peyton in the *Defence,* Gould in the *Audacious,* and, a little later, Thompson in the little *Leander,* 50 guns. Troubridge carried the all-important orders. You will notice that these are all fighting ships, that there are no frigates, the eyes of the fleet. The fact was that St. Vincent had only two frigates left to him, and these he could not spare—in any case, of course, he thought that Nelson was better off than himself in this respect, for Nelson had gone off to take a look into Toulon with three or four frigates.

But by the time Troubridge found him he had lost the frigates, had, in fact, almost lost more, almost lost his flagship, almost lost his life.

Was this to be the end of all his glory?

He had sailed from Gibraltar on May 9, with four frigates, a sloop, the *Vanguard,* of course, and two other ships of the line, the *Orion,* commanded by Sir James Saumarez, a brilliant fighter from the Channel Islands, and the *Alexander,* commanded by a tall, tranquil captain from Gloucestershire, Captain Ball. Now Ball's record as far as both seamanship and fighting were concerned was equal to that of Saumarez, and any admiral would, one supposes, be delighted to have such a captain in his squadron. But not Nelson, of elephantine memory, Nelson who remembered a trip to France in the autumn of 1783, when he had seen a brother officer—

Captain Alexander Ball—seen, but never exchanged a word with him, for the very sight of Ball had been enough to make him quite certain that he could feel nothing but detestation for a man everyone else held in high esteem. Why? Because, on his uniform coat, Alexander Ball wore *epaulettes*. Epaulettes—the very word denotes a French origin, of course; epaulettes, worn by French naval officers in 1783, but not by British.

In the years between the first unfortunate encounter and the second, epaulettes had as a matter of fact become an established part of the British naval officer's uniform; Nelson himself was wearing them when he received Ball with what one of his first biographers was to call "coolness," but this fact was of trivial importance in Nelson's eye; *nothing*, he vowed, could ever efface that first impression. That such a man could be placed under his command!

Eleven days later he thanked God that such a man had been sent to him. On the 19th, when they were in the Gulf of Lyons, dreaded for its violent gales, a storm hit them. It moderated a little on the 20th, but after dark struck again with renewed violence. Now the *Vanguard* was newly constructed, with a raw, unhandy crew. Just before midnight her main-topmast went over the side, and shortly afterwards the mizzen-topmast. The storm was so great that no signal could be seen, or heard. At half past three the foremast went in three pieces, and the bowsprit was sprung in three places. Dawn showed the little squadron dispersed; the frigates were gone no man knew where, the flagship was dismasted, so helpless that the appearance of a single enemy frigate would have created terror or despair, and she was drifting, drifting towards the rocky shores of Corsica.

But *Alexander* remained. *Alexander* took the crippled flagship in tow, hoping to get her safely to a Sardinian harbor.

71

You may imagine the risks this meant for *Alexander;* Nelson knew these risks, and ordered *Alexander* to cast off. Ball, unreliable Ball whom no man of sense would trust, replied calmly that with Sir Horatio's permission, he would stay with him, and with God's help save the *Vanguard.*

And save her he did. Nelson at the first opportunity boarded the *Alexander,* hugged Ball, and said, "A friend in need is a friend indeed!" Never was the trite old saying so true. Now in place of coolness came warmth, and there was never to be any feeling save the sincerest friendship and admiration for "my dear Ball."

The end of the episode shows Nelson at his best, just as the beginning, with the harping on old grievances, shows him at his most childish and irritating. But if we really want to see that better, that *real* Nelson, with that deep humility and God-fearing quality so many people never detected, let us read the letter he wrote to his wife, describing the storm:

"I ought not to call what has happened to the *Vanguard* by the cold name of accident; I believe firmly it was the Almighty's goodness, to check my consummate vanity. I hope it has made me a better officer, as I feel confident it has made me a better man. Figure to yourself, on Sunday evening, at sunset, a vain man walking in his cabin, with a squadron around him, who looked up to their chief to lead them to glory. Figure to yourself, on Monday morning, when the sun rose, this proud man, his ship dismasted, his fleet dispersed, and himself in such distress that the meanest frigate out of France would have been an unwelcome guest . . ."

There was, at least, one torment he was spared on that black night of storm and terror—he did not know that when

Vanguard was fighting for her life, the French fleet had sailed from Toulon, and had passed within a few miles of the little squadron.

It was from a neutral vessel that Nelson learned on May 27 exactly how much the storm had cost him, for the enemy fleet and a host of transports had got out of Toulon. As to *where* it had gone, he could only use his own judgment. He might be able to pick up a piece or two of the jigsaw puzzle here and there, but mostly he would have to act on guess-work—or inspiration. Troubridge had by this time joined him, but though he had a battle fleet, he had no frigates for scouting work.

And the wind fell calm, dead calm.

By the time Nelson could take up the chase, the enemy had a two weeks' start. Anything might have happened.

The first scrap of information came from the villainous-looking commander of a Barbary pirate craft, and even this was not first-hand, merely that on June 10 he had spoken to the captain of a Greek ship, who had described how six days before he had passed through a great fleet of two hundred sail—sailing east.

Some commanders, with a dozen ships at their disposal, might have pondered dolefully on such odds, but all that Nelson could think was that at last he had been given a scent, now he could run the enemy down, and run him down he would, he resolved, even if it meant sailing to the ends of the earth.

They were off the coast of Italy then. The gigantic Hardy had joined Nelson now in the little brig, *Mutine*. Nelson sent him off with Troubridge to Naples, to get what information he could, to ask the Neapolitan court to open the ports of the kingdom to the British ships, but above all, to get frigates from the Neapolitans—if the French were to be tracked down, Nelson had to have frigates. True, from the moment he had heard that the enemy had been sailing eastward, he had believed their destination was India, but frigates he must have to make a guess certainty.

Troubridge came back empty-handed; the King of Naples would give neither frigates nor permission to enter the ports of his kingdom. But on June 22 the *Mutine* learned from a Genoese brig that the French had captured Malta and had gone on eastward.

So the enemy goal was Egypt, after all, and Nelson had been right when, some days before, he had written to the First Lord of the Admiralty that if the enemy sailed past Sicily, their immediate objective would be Alexandria, their ultimate aim, India.

He called his captains to a council, put before them all the information at his disposal, told them what conclusions he had drawn, asked them if they agreed. They did—the capture of the stepping-stone, Malta, the size of the enemy expedition, the direction of the wind—all pointed to Egypt. Nelson calculated that at that moment they were actually approaching Alexandria.

He was right—and wrong. The information brought by Hardy had been right and wrong—had fatally misled him. The enemy had captured Malta, but had not sailed on directly. They had remained there until the 19th, so that when Nelson, three days out in calculations—made in the mistaken belief that the enemy had sailed on the 16th—thought they were at Alexandria, they were really close at hand, *so close at hand, in fact, that on the 22nd, his lookouts saw the sails of French frigates on the far horizon. But, fatally misled by the false information, Nelson concluded that they could not belong to the main enemy fleet, for that had left Malta six days before . . .*

Frigates might have sped off over the dancing waves and told him the truth, but he had no frigates.

Night fell on that tragic 22nd of June, and with the darkness came mist. The British ships sailed in a swift, compact group, ready to attack the enemy when they were encountered, and in order to keep that formation as they fled through the blackness and murk, they fired minute guns. That night they came upon the French Fleet, but the firing warned the enemy admiral. Hastily he drew his ships off northward, in the direction of Crete, but it was a near thing. Only half an hour after the terrified enemy had disappeared over the horizon, the sun rose. Had dawn come thirty minutes sooner, the history of the world would have been altered; Nelson's ships would have been in among the transports like famished wolves on silly sheep, it would have been the end of the expedition, the end of Bonaparte, there would have been no Trafalgar, no Austerlitz, no Waterloo.

For six days more Nelson and his captains believed the enemy were ahead of them, for six days more they pressed forward, all sails spread, beneath a blazing sky over a blue sea so empty that on the way they encountered only three vessels, two from Alexandria and one from the Archipelago; none of them had seen the French. Yet the enemy *must* be Egypt-bound—where else would they go after taking Malta? With any luck the British would come upon the enemy in Alexandria in the very act of disembarkation.

But when they reached Alexandria, hoping, as Captain Saumarez put it, to be relieved of their "cruel suspense," they found no sign of the enemy, no news concerning them.

Even this dreadful shock did not make Nelson doubt the information that had so terribly misled him. Therefore, still believing that the enemy had left Malta on the 16th, still calculating that the expedition must have covered a certain distance in the days that had elapsed, he thought that there must have been a landing in Syria, or in the Dardanelles—in other words, he mistrusted not the information, but his own judgment. In a fever of anxiety, an agony of remorse because he had guessed the wrong destination, he set sail at once for the north. Not a moment was to be wasted; he would not wait for an instant in Alexandria.

If he had been less afire to get to grips with the enemy, if he had waited for only a few hours, he would have had them, the enemy fleet, the best army in France, and Bonaparte too. Bonaparte came to Alexandria on the same day that Nelson left it. Again a handful of frigates would have altered the history of the world.

So Bonaparte proceeded to the conquest of Egypt, stormed first Alexandria, then Cairo, wiped out the defending army in the shadow of the Pyramids, while Nelson——?

He was scouring the shores of Syria, Asia Minor, Greece, endlessly, fruitlessly, in search of the enemy, but there was no sight of them, no sound of them. All this would have been torturing enough to an officer not over-sensitive, but the thin-skinned Nelson, his imagination working overtime, thought endlessly through the sultry days and breathless nights of what they were saying of him in England, how they were attacking St. Vincent, who had made enemies enough by giving him his command. It was only in writing to St. Vincent that he could ease his mind a little in the long, long days, when they beat back to the central Mediterranean in the face of a westerly wind, wondering all the while if Sicily *had* been attacked after all, since it seemed clear the French had not come into the Levant.

On July 19, they were back at Sicily, at Syracuse, with their water nearly exhausted, and the cowardly Neapolitan government still too scared of the French to give open help. Nelson was almost desperate. The devil's children, meaning the French, had the devil's luck, he said wearily. He still had no clue where they had gone.

On the 25th, he sailed east again. Somewhere in those waters the enemy must be, and if his ships were above water, Nelson would find them.

He seemed calm enough, but at least the officers standing the night watches knew how feigned a thing that composure was, that the admiral was sleepless, called on them time and time again to know the hour, could not believe that it was not yet daybreak, so interminable were the nights.

He said, years later, to Troubridge, "Don't fret . . . I wish I never had." The return to Syracuse, he thought, had broken his heart.

But the fretting and heartbreak, the sleepless nights were all speedily drawing to a close. On the 28th, three days after leaving Syracuse, there was news, news from Greek fishermen of a great fleet seen a month before, a fleet so great that it had spread far over the seas. And that fleet had been making for Egypt after all!

On July 1, Bonaparte had landed in Egypt; on August 1, the British fleet came in sight of Alexandria a second time. And again there was no French fleet in sight.

But a French tricolor was flying over the town.

Yet that made things no better. Bonaparte must have landed his army and sent his fleet back to France. It did not help to know that they had been right in seeking Alexandria, when on the first occasion they had come too early, and now they had come too late.

It was now about noon. Sick at heart, they followed the routine that they had followed more than a month before—turned east, and began sailing along the coast, three, six, nine, ten miles, and the officers sat down to eat with small appetite, twelve miles, fifteen miles—and there, fifteen miles to the east lay the French fleet, moored in line of battle.

Fighting Stations, Aboukir Bay

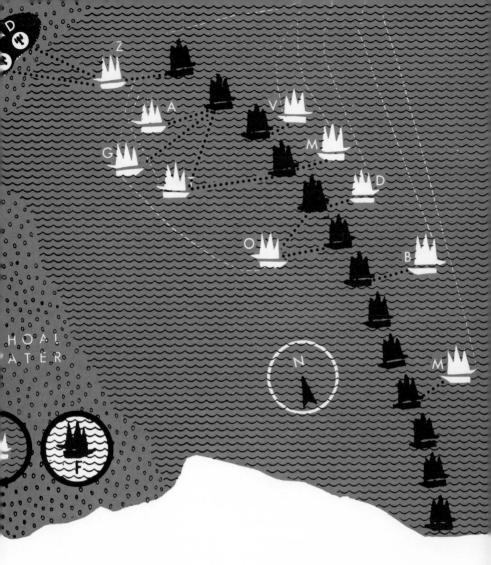

In one of his letters, the French admiral, De Brueys, had written that it was his private belief that the British had missed him, because, not being superior in force, they did not think it wise to meet him. Therefore, when one of his first rates signalled, in rapid succession about two o'clock, "Strange sail in sight," "Enemy in sight," and "Enemy moving on the bay," the admiral was not seriously alarmed. As his commissary of the fleet said, his vessels were moored in such a manner as to bid defiance to a force more than double his own, and the approaching fleet was anything but this. In any case, he did not believe there would be a battle that night; night falls fast in tropical waters, the British would come into the bay with the twilight, and only madmen would attempt a night action in uncharted waters! De Brueys was pretty sure they had no native pilots; he himself, on the orders of Bonaparte, had offered a reward of 10,000 livres (equal to about 10000 pounds of silver) to any Egyptian pilot who would carry his squadron in, but for all the reward offered, no pilot could be found skilled and daring enough to take in a single vessel drawing more than twenty feet.

What then was the position the French admiral believed to be impregnable? His fleet lay in Aboukir Bay, sandy-shored, and protected by shallows and rocks, with shoals to the eastward, and at the western end, Aboukir Island, with its guns. The sixteen French ships lay in a great crescent northwest to southeast near two miles long, with 160 yards between each ship. They mounted 1,196 guns in all; the head of the line was protected by Aboukir Island with its batteries of mortars. In the enemy center lay the flagship, the lovely giant called *L'Orient* with 120 guns; the center was indeed the strongest, with the rear next in strength.

De Brueys did not realize that he was fighting no ordinary enemy, but the supreme fighter in the history of all sea warfare, the admiral to whom nothing seemed impossible. (But his subordinate, Admiral Pierre Charles Villeneuve was to realize it, and was to be haunted by that knowledge for the rest of his days.)

And the British fleet came steadily in from the west with all sails spread. Shortly the blood-red sun would set behind them. Before it rose again, Nelson's fate would be decided; either he would have suffered the last disaster, or he would have triumphed. He himself had no doubts as to the answer. Captain Berry had said, "If we succeed, what will the world

80

say?" and Nelson had replied tranquilly, "There is no *if* in the case, that we shall succeed is certain." But he had added soberly, "Who will live to tell the story is a very different question."

Nelson saw how the enemy strength lay in the center, that the part of the line next in strength was the rear—therefore the enemy van was the point of weakness. In the discussions he had had with his captains he had always said that if he found the enemy at anchor, he would concentrate his attack on part of the line, and destroy it before the other enemy ships could come to its aid. Obviously the van was the place to attack. That meant bringing his fleet round inside the island, passing between it and the leading ships—and all this as darkness fell, and with no chart of the bay save a rough sketch taken by Captain Hallowell out of a prize. Still, his ships could go in sounding as they went, and as for the darkness—just time to get round the island before it was night—well, his captains knew what was in his mind, and elaborate signals were quite superfluous. Their fighting stations? Why, where there was room for an enemy ship to swing, there was room for one of his own ships to anchor.

He made, in all, three signals.

To form line of battle in order of sailing.

Each ship was to hoist four lights at the mizzen peak, (This was because three of his ships, *Swiftsure, Alexander* and *Culloden,* being miles astern, could not join in the action before it was completely dark, and there must be some way of distinguishing friend from foe.)

On reaching her allotted station, each ship was to anchor by the stern instead of by the head. (This killed two birds with one stone. Not only would she be in a position to commence fighting immediately, but she denied the enemy the opportunity of raking her as her bows swung round into the wind.)

81

Now his ships slipped into line, the *Goliath* in the lead. The *Vanguard* herself fell back to the center of the line— an essential position for Nelson to be able to keep control of the fighting, to observe what progress his leaders were making, and use the rest of his fleet as the situation demanded.

Meanwhile, the French feeling of easy confidence had evaporated; in the first place, the enemy was, incredibly, bent on coming into this unknown bay and fighting an action in the darkness, and in the second place as the waiting moments passed, officers remembered certain facts that caused uneasy stirrings in their minds . . . decks cluttered up with stores . . . crews whose lack of training was equalled only by their lack of discipline . . . and even those crews were not all aboard their ships at the moment, for many had been sent ashore, some to dig wells, others to protect the well-diggers from the hostile Arabs—those same Arabs who now came crowding to line the shores of the bay, to cheer the unknown saviors sweeping in with the night to rid them of their French oppressors, the impious infidel that had invaded without ever declaring war . . .

Unnerving to think that before midnight no French throat might be safe from the incensed Arabs.

There is one more fact to remember about the French fleet in general, and one fact more about the flagship, *L'Orient*, in particular. The enemy had thought themselves so safe on the shoreward side, with the protecting sandbanks, that they did not bother to clear the guns on that side, all cluttered up with stores as they were. So the port batteries were useless. As for *L'Orient*, they had been painting her sides when the avenging fleet had been sighted, and in the rush of preparation, jars of oil and buckets of paint, the most combustible things in the world, had been left lying about.

As the British fleet advanced, the French guns—that is, the starboard guns—opened fire, fire received in silence. The British line was led by the *Goliath,* which had won the lead from the *Zealous,* and the result of this jockeying for position was to be of the greatest importance, for the captain of the *Goliath,* Foley, had a modern atlas, a French atlas, with a good map in it. The captain of the *Zealous* had no chart at all, Nelson, as we know, had only a rough sketch out of a French prize, but Foley *had* a map, led the line masterfully, brilliantly, so assuredly as the dark red sun went down that one of the enemy officers, who was later captured, said afterwards he had been convinced the British had pilots after all. But Foley did more than lead the line; he gambled inspiredly on the idea that because of the way in which the French were moored, the guns on their shoreward side were not likely to be manned, or even ready for action. We know that he was right in this guess; we can see that from the moment Foley led the line to take up a position between the French ships and the shore, the battle was really won.

The action began at half past six. By seven, night had fallen completely, and the only light was the flash of the guns; it was too early for the moon to rise.

Foley rounded the head of the enemy line, swept past the undefended flank of the helpless French ships, poured in a broadside, took up his station, was followed by Hood in the *Zealous* (ten minutes it took Hood to disable the *Guerrier*), Saumarez in the *Orion,* Miller in *Theseus,* Gould in the *Audacious.*

Now it was the *Vanguard's* turn, and she, leading the rest of the fleet, took up her position on the *other* side of the French line. The time was now seven o'clock, the leading ships in the enemy line were being fired into from two sides by the British, while the vessels in the rear were forced to watch their comrades' destruction in awful helplessness, unable themselves to escape the ruin inevitably approaching them. Ten British ships were in action.

Of the remainder of Nelson's command, Troubridge in the *Culloden,* which had led the line at St. Vincent, had been two leagues astern. He had come up as fast as he could in the intense darkness, sounding as he came, but just as it seemed he might take part in the action, his vessel went aground, and stayed so throughout the night. You may imagine his heartbreak. Yet it would be wrong to say that the *Culloden* played no part at all in the battle, for at least her plight warned the other two ships hurrying astern of her to take care; but for her lights, the *Alexander* and the *Swiftsure* would have gone on to the reef. As it was, they safely achieved the infinitely difficult entrance into the bay; the *Swiftsure* encountered a strange sail as she sped into the fight, and any ship lacking the matchless discipline of Captain Hallowell's vessel might well have opened fire. But Hallowell ordered his men to hold their fire, for he thought the unknown vessel had the look of a British ship. He was right; she was the *Bellerophon,* drifting out of the fight after a duel with the giant enemy flagship, lights overboard, masts and cables shot away, nearly two hundred of her crew killed or wounded. The *Swiftsure* went in and took the place of her crippled comrade, two minutes later she opened up with her first great broadside, while Ball's *Alexander* passed under the flagships' stern, to rake him from the other side. Time, a few minutes past eight o'clock. A few minutes earlier, Nelson, standing on his quarter-deck, and peering down at the scrap of paper that was his chart, had been struck on the head by a piece of flying enemy scrap-shot.

They took him below to that nightmare place, the cockpit. The surgeon, on Nelson's entry, immediately left the task occupying him to attend to the admiral, but the admiral ordered him back. He would take his turn. So he waited, convinced he was a dying man, until all those wounded before him had been attended to, and then it was his turn, and, as the surgeon examined him, tense silence descended on the cockpit—only to be broken by cheers when the verdict was announced—the wound was *not* a mortal one.

The pain, however, was great, and the doctor said the admiral was to rest; he was not the first doctor to find Nelson a difficult patient. This much, though, should be said in Nelson's defense; a dispatch announcing victory (already three enemy vessels had been taken and three disabled) had to be composed as soon as possible, and Nelson's own secretary was too unnerved to write; there was nothing for it but for Nelson himself, swathed in bandages like a mummy, to seize a pen, and, in the breadroom of his flagship, blindly to start scrawling his news . . . "Almighty God has blessed His Majesty's arms . . ."

But then they brought him other news, news that brought him back up on deck, despite the surgeon's frantic protests.

Just under an hour after the *Swiftsure* had taken up her position—that is, about nine o'clock—Captain Hallowell saw flames leaping up from the enemy flagship, on the quarterdeck of which her admiral lay dead. The fire spread with dreadful speed, because of the paint and oil which lay about; soon it was great enough to illumine the bay to such an extent that the very colors of the ships' ensigns and battle flags could be picked out. As the flames roared towards the magazine of *L'Orient,* all ships that could drew away, all that is, save *Alexander,* made by Ball as fireproof as any wooden-walled warship could hope to be.

Nelson immediately ordered that the boats of his own flagship should be lowered to pick up survivors—more and more of the crew of *L'Orient* were hurling themselves into the sea. Only one boat remained undamaged, however, and one boat could not do much.

At about a quarter to ten the French flagship blew up with an explosion so terrible that the shock of it was felt at Rosetta ten miles away. One moment there was a great roar and a flame that made the wide bay as light as day; then there was utter darkness, utter silence as if that whole world of violence had come to an end. Firing immediately ceased on both sides, and the first sound that broke the awful hush was the noise of the fragments of the great ship striking the water as they rained down from a stupendous height. Of her crew about seventy were saved.

The moon arose to cast her brilliance over that scene of death and disaster, and firing began again, but the old fury had gone. Nelson was dazed by his wound, unable to go on directing operations; friend and foe alike were unnerved by the great explosion, and the British were—literally—almost dropping with fatigue. There had been the strain of the long chase, frantic sailing all that day, and then the fight. In the *Theseus* Captain Miller found his exhausted men falling asleep at their posts; in the *Alexander* the crew sent a deputation to Ball saying that though they wished to go on firing, they simply lacked the strength, so might they sleep for half an hour at their guns?

Even when dawn broke and they could see the six enemy vessels that had struck, the three dismasted ships aground or adrift, the charred wreckage that was all that remained of the proudest of flagships, they were too weary to understand how great a victory they had won. Only three French ships, those in the rear under the command of the horrified Villeneuve, still survived, and when they tried to escape one of them ran aground and her captain set her afire. It was only slowly that the conquerors realized that they had won the most complete of all naval victories . . . two thousand enemy dead, fifteen hundred wounded, two thousand prisoners, only two of the thirteen enemy battleships still at large.

Moreover, the whole European situation had been literally changed overnight; the victories resulting from Bonaparte's shameless aggression in Egypt were now nothing more than Dead Sea fruit. Before twilight fell on August 1, the French had held the Mediterranean, Egypt was the gateway to the conquest of the east. Before the sun rose again, they had lost control of the Mediterranean, and Egypt was transformed into a prison, for sand held them in to east and west and south, and sea to the north.

For three nights following the victory, the rejoicing Arabs lit bonfires along the coast, throughout the country; on the morning following the victory the uneasy French ashore noted a strange and mystifying stillness falling on the victorious fleet. The British, on the orders of their admiral, were returning thanksgiving in every ship to Almighty God.

News of the victory took two months and a day to reach England, but, of course, for weeks before it had been known that Nelson had lost the French fleet, at a time when Ireland was aflame with revolt. When the great news finally arrived, Lord Spencer, First Lord of the Admiralty, fell flat in the passage outside his office, and afterwards lay "stretched upon his couch, pale as death."

The victorious admiral (soon to be created Baron Nelson) had also been stretched on his couch (or cot), but, one might think, with better reason. His headwound, coming after the long months of strain, threw him into a fever, and, while his temperature soared, his head, he wrote to St. Vincent, was "splitting . . . splitting . . . splitting." When his fleet had licked its wounds, and was ready to put to sea again, the first port of call would be Naples, but Nelson hoped he would not have to stay there long, not more than four or five days, he wrote to the British Ambassador, Sir William

Hamilton, for he did not feel fit to cope with the court.

In actual fact, he was to spend about two years there, and at the end of that time had to be recalled, for he had remained "inactive at a foreign court" *while active service was proceeding in other parts of the station.*

Knowing Nelson, this charge seems incredible; judge then the feelings of the sad-eyed "band of brothers" who loved him, who had touched the topmost pinnacle of glory under his command, who were still under his command, *but carrying on the fight without him,* wondering in dull misery what had gone wrong.

The explanation lay in the fact that Nelson had spoken only too truly when he had said he was in no fit state to cope with the court of Naples. He was more or less shell-shocked; his poor dazed brain was unable to tell the difference between falsehood and sincerity. The court of Naples (which had almost broken his heart by its conduct when it seemed Bonaparte had made the Mediterranean a French lake) now loudly proclaimed him as its hero and savior; the ridiculous, cowardly king was even persuaded by Nelson to carry on the good work by driving out the French garrisons holding down the rest of Italy.

The campaign began—and soon ended. A Neapolitan army of 19,000 made contact with a French force of 3,000; one cannot say the Neapolitans were beaten, for they did not stay to fight. Everywhere the story was the same, and in the main army the king himself led the flight. "The Neapolitan officers," exploded Nelson, "did not lose much honor, for, God knows, they had not much to lose, but they lost all they had."

The king and his army had won the race back to the capital, but how long they would be permitted to remain there was a different story. Certainly the French would be out for revenge. The cowardly court panicked; it must leave Naples, where the enraged people might rise against it. Its only defense was Nelson's squadron, which must take it, with what treasure it could lay hands on, to Sicily—so conveniently an island. The people of Naples could be left to face the wrath of the French.

Standing guard over this contemptible court was not, of course, part of Nelson's duty; he should have been laying siege to Malta, or patrolling the coast of Egypt. He acted for nearly two years more like an officer in Neapolitan pay than a British admiral because he had come completely under the influence of the Hamiltons, who had taken him to their house in Naples to recover from his wound. In his gratitude, he thought them the best and wisest people alive; Lady Hamilton was the close friend of the Queen of Naples, and gradually Nelson came to see the court through her eyes. To preserve some of the most worthless wretches ever known, he sacrificed his own reputation.

When finally he was recalled, he, Britain's greatest sailor, went home by land. Most people thought him finished.

But a miracle happened. As he traveled north, further and further away from Naples, the old Nelson began to reappear. By the time he had crossed the North Sea, he was afire to serve again. But would the Admiralty want him? This time there would be reason enough for coldness.

But on this occasion Nelson was lucky. A new Commander-in-chief had been appointed to the Channel Fleet, and he requested that Nelson should serve under him. Lord St. Vincent had come back from the Mediterranean. He it was who had given Nelson his first great glittering chance, and a year later the best of his ships; now he was to give him an even greater chance—the chance to redeem himself and make amends, and when, within a few months, Nelson was transferred from the Channel Fleet and sent into the Baltic, he fought a battle that showed that the Italian nightmare was over, and that he was fully restored to the Navy.

Cautious Approach to Copenhagen

Nelson was appointed to the fleet being sent into the Baltic to deal with a new combination of enemies—Denmark, Sweden and Russia—which, under the leadership of Czar Paul of Russia, was threatening Britain. But he was not to command the expedition. In the eyes of the Admiralty, Nelson was a very juvenile officer, who *should* have been a most disastrous failure—only the confounded fellow was from time to time blessed with the most astounding luck. True, because of his popularity with the public, and the championship of old St. Vincent, he had to be employed in the expedition, but give him command of a fleet . . ! The very thought gave his superiors the horrors.

So for the sake of their nerves, Nelsons' superiors made him only second-in-command—and nearly ruined the expedition as a result. Sir Hyde Parker, appointed Nelson's chief in succession to St. Vincent, was very old, very rich, newly married to a young wife, and therefore, because of age and wealth and wife, very, very cautious. Sir Hyde did not want to risk his skin if he could help it.

Nelson, joining the fleet at Yarmouth in vile, blustery weather, found the old gentleman "a little nervous about dark nights and fields of ice." Nelson tried to galvanize him into action. "We must brace up," he said rousingly, "these are not times for nervous systems. I hope we shall give our northern enemies that hailstorm of bullets which gives our dear country the dominion of the sea. We have it, and all the devils in the north cannot take it from us if our wooden walls have fair play." Such sentiments, however, far from putting fresh life into Sir Hyde, positively paralyzed him with horror. He began to regard Nelson, daily bombarding him with entreaties to proceed, much as a sluggish and aging ox might regard a gadfly. Besides, his wife had just joined him, bent on tasting all the sweets of her position as admiral's wife; *she* talked of balls, and naval officers dancing in white gloves—far more soothing to an elderly gentleman than fiery words of hailstorms of bullets and northern devils. And then the outrageous Nelson really went too far. There were changes at the Admiralty; Lord St. Vincent, no less, was First Lord, and to him Nelson applied in despair to *goad* Sir Hyde into action. Down to Yarmouth, couched in the new First Lord's characteristic style, came sailing orders; Lady Parker did *not* have her ball, and Lady Parker raged; her devoted husband therefore set sail in the vilest humor with his second-in-command—which did not promise well for the coming campaign. Every time Lord Nelson submitted a written proposal, Sir Hyde simply struck it out with his pen.

Nelson had to make suggestions in writing because Sir Hyde remained sulkily in his flagship (and some of the worst weather in the North Sea within memory did not encourage a one-handed man to go paying calls in a small boat).

It was an impossible situation. In the country's interests, the old gentleman's favor *must* be won.

Naval tradition has it that the elderly admiral's hostility, roused by a cancelled ball, was lulled by the magical gift of a freshly caught flounder from a second-in-command who had gathered that food meant a great deal to his superior. Nelson followed up this shrewd stroke by paying a courtesy call on Sir Hyde, who unbent still further. It was not a moment too soon, for now there returned a diplomat, sent on ahead to negotiate with the Danes—he had not frightened the Danes, but the Danes had undoubtedly frightened him. He gave most alarming reports of the state of the enemy defenses; this had no effect on Nelson save to confirm him in his opinion that he hated "pen and ink men," but Sir Hyde was powerfully and unpleasantly impressed.

By this time Nelson had learned at some cost to himself several facts about his superior officer. One melancholy item was that if, after a persuasive-seeming interview, you left the old man believing you had won him round to your way of thinking, you were living in a fool's paradise; the moment your back was turned, his mind would veer round like a weathercock. So Nelson, despite himself, joined the ranks of the "pen and ink" men—literally so, for in order to keep Sir Hyde permanently converted, he had to keep sending him long and fiery letters. It is one of the oddest possible preludes to a battle—and shows the impetuous Nelson could on occasion have the patience of an angel.

Now such letters had two results, as far as Sir Hyde was concerned; in the first place, of course, when Nelson talked of England's honor being entrusted to him, it frightened him horribly, but in the second place, coming as he was more and more under the wand of the wizard, he was becoming even more horribly scared of being despised by Nelson. On the other hand, the pilots, cautious by nature and training, terrified by what they had heard of the Danish defenses, fought Nelson's proposal for a bold, direct approach to Copenhagen tooth and nail. Again Sir Hyde wavered.

But finally the Danish governor of Gronenburg Castle settled the matter. Sir Hyde had sent him a polite inquiry; would the governor tell him if he had received orders to fire at the British fleet? The governor, as might have been expected, replied that he could not allow a fleet the intentions of which were unknown, to approach the guns of the castle which he had the honor to command. Sir Hyde said in a stately manner that he had no choice but to interpret this answer as a declaration of war.

One cannot wonder that two young Danish officers, acting as messengers to Sir Hyde's flagship, boarded the *London* in a mood of defiance mingled with contempt. One, writing a note in Sir Hyde's Great Cabin, mortified the cabin's owner by calling out, "Admiral, if your guns are no better than your pens, you may as well return to England."

But their manner altered when they heard who sailed as second-in-command. The officer who had so poor opinion of Sir Hyde's pens showed now the keenest interest. "What, is he here? I would give a hundred guineas to see him!"

And then his mood changed again—this time to grimness. The British must mean business. "Then," he commented rather unkindly, looking at Sir Hyde, "I suppose it is no joke, if *he* is come!"

At this point Nelson shifted his flag from the *St. George* to the *Elephant*, commanded by an old friend, Captain Foley, who had led the line so brilliantly when it advanced into Aboukir Bay. The change of ship was made because the *Elephant*, a lighter ship than the *St. George*, was therefore more suited to the operations now planned. Now there followed another halt; for even if Nelson had managed to spur Sir Hyde into action, he could not order the wind—*that* did not come fair until March 30, and then the fleet advanced in order of battle, and in three divisions, Nelson's own in the van, Sir Hyde's in the center, Admiral Graves' in the rear.

It has been pointed out that the majority of great battles, whether on sea or on land, are fought in the neighborhood of unknown villages and capes, which henceforward are world famous. This was not the case in the Battle of the Baltic; it was fought in view of Copenhagen, one of the loveliest of the capitals of Europe, while only twenty miles from the capital lay Elsinore, a name familiar even to Englishmen who scarcely ever stirred from their libraries, for this was the scene of *Hamlet*.

Elsinore controls the Sound, and the Sound is the entrance to the Baltic. At the narrowest part, it is only three miles wide, and through this the British fleet must proceed. It seemed a grim prospect, and the ships advanced expecting to receive fire on the port side from the Swedish shore and on the starboard side from the Danes. Yet, miraculously, no shots whatsoever came from the Swedes; for once the luck was with Nelson, and he took full advantage of it, altering course so as to hug the harmless Swedish shore, bringing the fleet out of range of the hot fire from the Danes.

Within the next few days the fleet must deliberately seek a murderously close gun duel with the Danes—a prospect grim enough in itself, especially after an afternoon's reconnaissance had given Sir Hyde and his officers first-hand knowledge of the advantage taken by the Danes by the incessant British delays to strengthen their defenses, but far worse when one bore in mind that the Danes were only the first of three enemies that had to be encountered, and that the other two, the Swedes and Russians, might come into sight during the very engagement. At the council of war held after the reconnaissance, some officers kept stressing this point. But Nelson, striding impatiently up and down, brushed aside their arguments for caution: "The more numerous, the better: I wish they were twice as many," he said cheerfully, "the easier the victory, depend on it."

What were the obstacles the British fleet must overcome? A line of ships, gunboats, batteries nearly four miles long, a difficult channel to be negotiated before the defenses could be attacked at all—in fact, so hazardous was the passage of the channel at any time that the Danes, now that the guiding buoys had been removed, scarcely thought the enemy fleet could make the passage at all.

So again there was delay, though this was necessary—and laborious beyond belief. It was toil day and night, taking soundings in small boats, setting fresh buoys into position, all in freezing cold. Nelson himself considered this the worst part of his task—it wore him down, he said, and he found it harder to endure than any amount of enemy resistance.

The wind being southerly, it was decided to make the attack from the south, Nelson wishing to attack the moment he had a fair wind. But now it is time to look at the precautions for defense made by the Danes.

In the first place, of course, they had powerful natural defenses, not only the intricate channel which was the sole approach, but a great shoal called the Middle Ground, lying some three-quarters of a mile before the capital, and stretching along the entire length of the sea front. Between the shoal and the town lay the deep water of the King's Channel, and here, and as near the shore as possible, the Danes had set up their defenses, nineteen ships and floating batteries with, at the end nearest the capital and most formidable of all, two artificial islands called the Crown batteries, the larger one of which had sixty-six guns.

Gun Duel in the Baltic

On the chilly April night before the attack, all his captains dined with Nelson, drank to success the next day, then returned to their ships, save for Riou, the heroic officer in command of the light craft, who remained behind for a last discussion of plans, and Hardy, largest of men, who was now out in a small boat—a gigantic cloaked figure, examining the channel between British and Danes, approaching so near that he actually sounded round the leading Danish ship (using a pole, for the tiny splash made by throwing the lead might betray him). He reported his findings at eleven o'clock; Nelson was by this time lying in a cot, being so worn out by keeping body and mind on the stretch for the past three days that he had allowed himself to give way to the genial bullying of his servant, Allen, and lie down. But not to sleep, of course. Until one in the morning he was dictating orders from his cot—there must be no possible misunderstandings on the part of his captains—and even after the dictation was ended, he did not sleep, waiting anxiously for the news that the wind was turning fair.

By daybreak he heard what he wanted, by six he had got up, breakfasted, and made a signal that all captains should come aboard for final orders. Between eight and nine the signal was being made for pilots and masters—and now Nelson took a step he soon bitterly regretted. He had Hardy's report on the depth of the channel, but thought it wiser to trust instead to the pilots, who were nearly all former mates in ships plying the Baltic trade. Now, with the signal for action given, and the wind fair, he was to find that the pilots not only lacked real knowledge of the shoals and channels, but had lost their nerve. At length Brierly, master of the *Bellona,* and a veteran of the Nile, volunteered to lead the fleet, and at half past nine the attack began.

The line was led by the *Edgar,* followed by the *Agamemnon,* and we can imagine Nelson's dismay when the *Agamemnon* went aground on the edge of the shoal. Time was everything; immediately he signalled to the *Polyphemus* to take *Agamemnon's* place, but, swiftly though his order was obeyed, there was inevitably some delay; in this campaign of delays there was a very bad period in which the *Edgar* was totally unsupported, and even when *Polyphemus* did come up, the intricacy of the channel kept her from occupying the berth planned for her by Nelson.

But the *Isis,* next in line, did all that was expected of her;

men began to breathe again, and hope that the spell of bad luck was over—but worse disasters were in store. The *Bellona*, next to advance, grounded on the starboard shoal, as also did the *Russell*, following her. So of six ships, only two had taken up the positions planned for them; it seemed as if all Nelsons' plans would come to ruin, but luckily the seventh ship in the line was the *Elephant*, flying his own flag—and he was very much in command of the situation. He saved the flagship itself by ordering her helm to starboard, that is, he passed to *port* of the grounded ships, between them and the enemy line, thus gaining fairly deep water, safely threaded his way through the channel, and took up the berth originally intended for the *Bellona*. Moreover, by this action, he saved not only his own flagship, but the vessels following her, who took her as their guide.

But if the rest of the fleet was saved from going aground, damage enough had been done; Nelson had planned to use twelve ships in the attack, but now he had only nine.

Fighting had begun at five past ten, and an hour and a half afterwards all the British ships available were engaged. The original plan had become terribly disorganized, but at least two officers were anything but demoralized; Captain Riou calmly took his light craft to attempt the task assigned to the guns of three sail of the line—a duel against the immensely strong Crown Battery, while Nelson himself, aghast as he must have been when he realized that a quarter of his force was useless, found in the thunder of a thousand enemy guns a perfect cure for all anxiety. Action always acted on him like a tonic.

But with Sir Hyde, things were different. It had been agreed that he, with the remainder of the fleet, was to appear from the north, to menace and demoralize the Danes, but the wind that was fair for Nelson was, of course, foul for his superior, who therefore approached the scene of action later than had been planned, and by half past one was still too far away to be of any positive assistance. He could, however *see* something of what was going on—that, for example, accidents had seriously weakened Nelson and he could also hear that the Danish fire was far heavier than had been expected. Sir Hyde, bearing in mind these two things—Nelson's weakened force, the unexpected strength of the Danish resistance—judged that the position was hopeless, and made a signal to leave off action.

It was Signal No. 39. By the time it was hoisted, Nelson's mood was one of enormous cheerfulness. In great exhilaration, he was pacing the quarter-deck, observing that it was warm work, and swearing, like a ninth-century Viking, that he would not be elsewhere for thousands. Hardly the right spirit for receiving an order to discontinue the action! In fact, when the *Elephant's* signal officer reported it to him, he went on pacing the deck without apparently taking any notice. The lieutenant, thinking he had not heard, met him at the next turn, and asked if he should repeat it (to the other ships in the squadron). "No," said Nelson, "merely acknowledge it." A moment later he called after the lieutenant—and here he showed far more feeling—was his own signal, for close action, still hoisted? Hearing it was, he said grimly, "Mind you keep it so!"

There was silence for some moments as he went on pacing up and down, but those who knew him well could see, from the way he was moving the stump of his arm, that he was very excited. Then he turned to a military officer.

"Do you know what is shown on board the commander-in-chief? No. 39!"

"What does that mean, sir?"

"Why, to leave off action . . ! Leave off action! Now blast me if I do!" He turned to the captain and brought up the glass to his blind eye—more in bitterness than in the playful way so often described to us. "You know, Foley, I have only one eye, I have a right to be blind sometimes: I really do not see the signal . . . Blast the signal! Keep *mine* for closer battle flying! That's the way I answer such signals. Nail mine to the mast!"

And the other ships of the line, looking to him for orders, disregarded the flagship's signal.

Riou, however, with the frigates, was nearest the commander-in-chief, obeyed the signal, and in withdrawing from before the battery, was killed by a raking shot. The Navy could have spared him least of all officers save one—and that exception was Nelson.

So the battle went on, waged as determinedly and bravely by the defenders as by their assailants, but at last the Danish fire began to slacken. The effort was so great it could not be kept up for an unlimited time; by two o'clock nearly all the Danish guns were silent. Nelson immediately seized the chance of ending the murderous conflict; he did not hate the Danes, gallant and honorable enemies, closely related to the English by blood—was not his own name proof of this? Britain's danger had made the attack necessary, but now that the Danes could no longer threaten, let there be an end to the fighting! Nelson ran down to the stern gallery, seized a pen, and began to write, "Vice-Admiral Nelson has been commanded to spare Denmark, when she no longer resists. . . . The brave Danes are the brothers, and should never be the enemies, of the English."

Thus, after four hours, the fighting ended, and after some discussion a truce was agreed upon, to last at first for twenty-four hours. Under a sky suddenly overcast, the British ships limped slowly back along the treacherous channel. Nelson, exhausted after his labors of the past days, was deeply depressed by the loss of life, British and Danish, and now, of course, he must go to face a superior officer whose orders he had disobeyed. True, his defiance had led to victory, but that very fact might make his offense quite unpardonable. Sir Hyde might find it easier to forgive him if he had been defeated, for by winning Nelson had made his superior look a timorous fool.

"Well," said the culprit, as he left his own ship, "I have fought contrary to orders, and I shall, perhaps, be hanged. Never mind: let them!"

But Sir Hyde did not, after all, order Nelson to be strung up at the yardarm. Also—and this is a point frequently overlooked, Nelson had a decided talent for diplomacy. Therefore he was commissioned to go ashore in due course to start talks with the Danish Crown Prince about a more lasting armistice.

To do this he landed, with only two companions, at a dangerous moment, for the men wounded in the defense of their capital were still being brought ashore, and the Danish authorities, fearing for Nelson's safety, gave him a strong escort. They should have known their countrymen better.

"The Admiral," said one of those he had defeated, "was received as one brave enemy ought to receive another—he was received with respect."

And Nelson himself, speaking to the Crown Prince, said that he had been in one hundred and five engagements, but this last had been the most tremendous of all.

"The French fought bravely, but they could not have stood for one hour the fight which the Danes had supported for four."

At last the armistice was concluded, and Nelson (created a viscount when the news of his victory reached home) was free to enter the Baltic with the aim of knocking out the leading spirit in the alliance against her—Russia. But there was no more fighting in the Baltic campaign; news came that the Russian Emperor, who hated Britain, had been murdered. That meant the end of the threat from the north, for the new Emperor wanted peace.

But the change in Russian rulers had even greater results. Bonaparte, now dictator of France, had hoped great things would come from the northern alliance against his stubborn enemy, but now, with Denmark signing an armistice, and Russia wanting only peace, he could not see how Britain could be beaten *at present,* for he simply could not get at her. Of course, he would settle accounts with her at some future date, but first he must rebuild his fleets, increase his armies, free France from the stranglehold of the blockade. He would therefore make peace with Britain—at least, the stupid British would think it was peace, but Bonaparte regarded it only as a truce; let him raise fresh fleets, new armies, then he would plunge into war again, and this time Britain would be invaded, conquered, and reduced to her proper footing, a mere dependent of France like any of the other islands off the French coast.

The so-called Peace of Amiens signed by Britain and France lasted for precisely one year and sixteen days. Towards the end of May, 1803, Nelson sailed from Portsmouth to take command of the Mediterranean Fleet, happy in the knowledge that his flagship would be the *Victory,* and his flag-captain Captain Thomas Masterman Hardy.

When he reached Gibraltar, where no one even knew that the war had broken out again, he had already managed to catch a cold, and had been in a fever of anxiety during a slow voyage (the wind was foul) because he had feared that Bonaparte, the moment war had been declared, had sent his newly built squadrons to sea. But for close on two years, there was to be little real action—only the deadly monotonous grind of keeping watch on Toulon.

Mark that he was not *blockading* the French fleet; too often we are given the impression that his aim was to keep the enemy bottled up in harbor, that all the French wanted to do was to put to sea, and Nelson's nightmare was that they would come out and fight. Really, it was the other way about; French admirals showed no burning desire to go out and fight Nelson, but were eventually goaded into an action they personally regarded as suicide by furious letters sent from Paris—all rather like what had gone on when Nelson's namesake had held the bridge:

"But those behind cried, 'Forward!'

And those before cried, 'Back!'"

Nelson himself was constantly tempting the French to come out; the surest way of infuriating him was to assume that it was his wish that the French fleet stayed in port, and when the City of London actually conveyed to him a vote of thanks for his skill and perseverance in blockading Toulon so that the French were prevented from putting to sea, Nelson, after fourteen months spent in vain hopes that the enemy *would* come out, exploded into fury in his reply to the Lord Mayor. "I beg to inform your lordship that the port of Toulon has never been blockaded by me—quite the reverse. Every opportunity has been offered the enemy to put to sea, for it is there that we hope to realize the hopes and expectations of our country."

So wrote the admiral whose constant endeavour had been to bring to battle an enemy whose ships were "as fine as paint could make them," while the condition of his own ships he described as "crazy." The fact was that the Admiralty, thinking the peace signed with Bonaparte was genuine, had gone in for economy, and the dockyards, where ships were both refitted and repaired, were special targets.

Nor was this the only difficulty Nelson had to contend with. The fleet had been expecting to go home when war broke out. It had already been at sea for six months, depended on distant Malta, had no supplies, and was riddled with scurvy. Only three ships of the line might be called new, and there were not enough frigates. Nelson decided to send his ships into port in turn, so that they would be ready for continuous cruising throughout the winter. Grimly noting, "We are not very superior, if anything, in point of numbers," he resolved nevertheless to "keep a good lookout, both here and off Brest, and if I have the means, I shall try and fight one party or the other before they form a junction."

Here Nelson's use of two words, *Brest* and *junction,* gives the key to the basic plan for the French invasion of England. Napoleon—he is soon to make himself emperor, and use his first name only—might make alterations in details as time passed, but in main outline the scheme always remained the same; there must be a junction of French fleets to gain command of the Channel so that the great army being assembled at Boulogne might pass over in safety. Though Spain is later to join in the war, and Napoleon's ideas were to become more elaborate as the months passed, all depended on a link up between two French fleets, those from Toulon and Brest. Here again we are so dazzled with Nelson that we rarely give other officers due credit. Though we tend to think of the Trafalgar campaign—the campaign which decided whether or not England was to be invaded—as a kind of personal duel between Nelson and Napoleon, the fleet that was all-important as far as invasion was concerned was not the Mediterranean squadrons, but the vessels with which Admiral Cornwallis cruised off the western approaches.

Another mistaken idea is that Napoleon's invasion scheme was so entirely original that the Admiralty was absolutely in the dark as to his intentions and that the situation was only saved by occasional flashes of inspiration on Nelson's part. The truth of the matter was that only a Board of Admiralty composed of lunatics (and though Nelson called them a set of beasts he never called them a set of maniacs) would have been in the dark as to what was intended, for this was no new situation. Had not the Armada sailed from Spain to gain control of the Channel to bring over an army from the Low Countries? At the time of Nelson's birth had not Admiral Boscawen watched Toulon while Admiral Hawke watched Brest? But Napoleon chose now to suppose that the British would forget the past, as, with Spanish as well as French squadrons to play with, he worked out what may be described as a snowball strategy. The Toulon fleet was to get out, elude Nelson, drive off the British fleet watching Cartagena, link up with the Spanish ships there, sail on to Cadiz, repeat the process, then, linking up with the squadrons from Ferrol, Rochefort and Brest, take command of the Channel.

It was all beautifully logical, but, even *if* the snowball began rolling, all depended on the Admiralty becoming so flummoxed by threats and horrid warnings from across the Channel that it threw its traditional policy to the winds. And that it would never do. *Whatever* happened, western approaches would be held in force. Every British admiral knew what he was to do if the enemy fleet he was watching got out. First, of course, he was to try to bring it to battle, but if it eluded him, he was to bring up his ships with all speed to join Cornwallis' fleet off Ushant, and so strengthen *that*, the all-important fleet. Ushant has been called "the center of gravity of British naval defense," and Cornwallis' command was the command that mattered above all others. If Cornwallis were defeated, only the much smaller squadron covering the Texel would be left; when that was dealt with, only the weather stood between Napoleon and conquest. The weather, of course, had done much to destroy the Armada, but one could not hope for a miracle to happen twice.

Yet would it ever come to depending on the weather alone for defense against invasion? If the French *did* make their link-up, they would find the approaches to the Channel held in strength by a great force *concentrated there almost automatically for the simple reason that they, the French, had got out.*

Cornwallis is unlucky, because he never fought a big battle. The fight that should have been his fell to Calder, who bungled it; it would have been a far different story if Cornwallis had met the combined fleets, for it was he who, twenty-five years before, had impressed upon a younger officer four essential facts that Nelson gratefully acknowledged:

"That you can always beat a Frenchman if you fight him long enough."

"That the difficulty of getting at them is sometimes more fancy than fact."

"That people never know what they can do until they have tried."

"When in doubt, to fight is always to err on the right side."

So do not forget Cornwallis even when Nelson himself gets the second chance of fighting the Combined Fleets after Villeneuve, though ordered north again by Napoleon, so lost his nerve that he crept south instead, and took refuge in Cadiz. There is a strange inevitability about it; Villeneuve fled west from Nelson, dared not linger in the West Indies because of Nelson—and yet, at the end, must meet Nelson after all, just as fated Greek princes of legend strove in vain to escape the doom ordained for them.

But we are looking forward. The British vessels are still

watching and waiting off the coasts of France and occupied Europe, and in Britain itself the threatened islanders strain their eyes for the firing of the invasion beacons—smoke signals by day, bright flame by night. They hear that the invading host will number one-hundred-seventy-five thousand veterans. In Britain itself all males between sixteen and sixty would be required to defend their homes. Napoleon was so confident of victory that already he had had his victory medal struck—Hercules (himself) strangling a sea-monster. The inscription actually read "Struck in *London*." Now all that Napoleon needed was a favorable wind, and command of the Channel for thirty-six hours . . . or twenty-four might be enough . . . or even twelve . . .

But to win that command, the French fleets must come out and link up—and the first to break out must be the fleet at Toulon.

The fleet that had been preyed upon by scurvy soon felt the benefit of being commanded by a man who did all he could to ensure constant supplies of fresh greens, oranges, lemons and onions. Within three months of taking over command, Nelson could report, "We are healthy beyond example, and in great good humor with ourselves, and so sharp set that I would not be a French Admiral . . ." He had in that short time overcome not only ill health but any ill humor felt by officers and men who before his coming had longed only to return home. Yet there remained one feat that even he could not achieve. That was the repair and refitting of ships kept too long at sea and which must remain at sea now. "I know well enough," he said, "that if I were to go into Malta, I should save the ships during this bad season, but if I am to watch the French, I must be at sea, and if at sea, must have bad weather." His first resolve had been, "Never to go into port till after the battle, if they make me wait a year, *provided the Admiralty change the ships who cannot keep the sea in winter.*" When, at the approach of winter, the Admiralty told him it could send out neither fresh ships nor fresh men, he would not give up his station. Even with his "crazy" ships, he would maintain his vigil.

Weary Sea Chase

Too often, now that the age of sail is over, we think of the Mediterranean as a place for comfortable pleasure voyages (though anyone who has read of the wanderings of Ulysses should know better), while as for the coast of Southern France, off which Nelson waited—why, travel posters give the idea that nothing could be more enjoyable than to spend the winter months cruising off the Riviera, Europe's winter-garden. Certainly the mountains deprive what has been called "this hot greenhouse shelf" of all normal wind, so that in the summer, particularly, the air seems absolutely stationary, with only the faintest sea breeze reaching the shore in the afternoon; but if you look seaward, there are all manner of signs that further out a stiff wind is blowing. In the distance there is a sickening swell, and out there, when a storm breaks, it breaks suddenly, and with terrifying violence. Even in summer, said Nelson, they had a gale off Toulon every week, while in winter the gales were incessant —and he added pathetically to an old friend, "you know I am never well when it blows hard." He was indeed, as he confessed to St. Vincent, "dreadfully seasick." Yet the chief enemy his fleet had to contend with was the deadly monotony of it all. "We cruise, cruise, and one day so much like another that they are hardly distinguishable . . ." Yet he kept his fleet happy, as he kept it healthy. Men might never set eyes on him, but they were assured of his affection for them, his interest in them, his hatred of harsh punishment (he used to say there was no need for him "to ruin a poor devil, who was sufficiently his own enemy to ruin himself"). And he felt delight in giving promotion to those who deserved it. There was, for example, a midshipman in the *Victory* who had risked his life to save a man who had fallen overboard, and was promoted lieutenant—"But mind," said Nelson gravely, "I'll have no more lieutenants for men falling overboard," a necessary warning, perhaps, or the Mediterranean might have been black with the bobbing heads of men that ambitious young gentlemen had induced by fair means or foul to fall into the sea.

As in 1798, Nelson lacked an adequate frigate force to watch the enemy; also as in 1798, he knew a sudden storm that scattered his own ships might be seized by the enemy as an opportunity to come out undetected. If the French came out, where would they go? Despite the invasion threat, Nelson could not be sure; Napoleon's past record showed that while his ambitions were boundless, his conscience was nonexistent, and so, as in 1798, he might again without any warning attack a country at peace with France. Thus, Nelson realized grimly, the Toulon fleet might have "as many destinations as there were countries." All that he could do was to keep his fleet well provisioned, and resolve to follow the enemy to the Antipodes if necessary. Not surprisingly, his thoughts kept returning to the burning summer of 1798, and the long search. If he missed the enemy again, he said his heart would break.

But he was not the only person remembering the summer of 1798. At the outbreak of war a new commander-in-chief had come to the Toulon fleet, and he too was obsessed by that campaign—but by the end of it, not the chase. Vice-Admiral Villeneuve had commanded one of the few French ships to escape the catastrophe. Napoleon, for this reason, thought him a "lucky" man, and so in due course gave him command of the Toulon fleet. But lucky? Villeneuve might have got away from the ruin that overwhelmed the rest of the French fleet, but not until he had seen the British admiral achieving what they had all thought impossible, and the most dreadful destruction ever known overtaking his helpless comrades. Villeneuve's *mind* never escaped from Aboukir Bay; thoughts of Nelson had haunted him ever since; as a British captain who met him was to tell Nelson, "Your lordship haunts his dreams." Such an admiral, brave and intelligent as he was, was half-defeated before ever he put to sea.

As for the admiral who *was* at sea, he was praying that he might be allowed to fight one more battle; he had grave doubts as to his health, but above all he feared total blindness, for one eye had to do the work of two in the harsh Mediterranean glare. "However," he said, "I have run a glorious race."

In the north of France, all roads led to Boulogne where the Grand Army was waiting to embark; from Paris Napoleon sent to the French and Spanish squadrons the orders that, he believed, would baffle the British commanders and scatter them to all quarters of the globe on wild-goose chases while the French and Spanish fleets combined, then sailed in overwhelming strength to gain control of the Channel. Villeneuve was to come out of Toulon, link up with the Spanish ships in Cadiz and Cartagena, sail across to the West Indies, selected as the rendezvous, and here he would unite with the other French squadrons which had broken out simultaneously from west-coast ports. Together they would return in triumph to western approaches, release the Brest fleet, annihilate the astounded Cornwallis, hold the Channel, and Napoleon would, in his own phrase, "leap the ditch."

But "leaping the ditch" depended on two things. Cornwallis must be left unsupported, whereas, as we have seen, all British admirals knew that if the squadrons they were watching managed to escape, they must fall back on the Channel mouth. No one, and, above all, Nelson, must guess where Villeneuve had gone. To help in the mystification, Napoleon ordered false reports to be put in the French newspapers, suggesting Egypt was to be invaded again. Villeneuve *must* disappear into the blue, and he *must* keep his rendezvous in the West Indies with the other French squadrons. Also—though this did not appear in official orders—Villeneuve must possess nerves of iron, which was precisely what he did not have. Poor "lucky" Villeneuve, brave and intelligent without question—too intelligent for his own peace of mind—of all tasks *he* must be given the task of confronting the admiral he regarded as a superhuman being, and this with a fleet the state of which would have depressed even an optimistic man.

He discovered the dreadful defects at the very beginning

of 1805. In January he obeyed the stream of orders coming from Napoleon and put to sea. The weather was bad, and the French ships simply did not know how to ride out the storm, being, as their unfortunate admiral put it, "harbor-trained." The damage sustained was, in fact, so bad that Villeneuve turned tail, and made his way back to Toulon, to the intense rage of Napoleon, who fumed that the great evil of his navy was that its officers were "unused to all the risks of command." True, of course—yet hardly strange in a fleet that rarely went to sea.

As for Nelson, once more the bad weather lost the French for him; he beat about in feverish haste, sailed to Sardinia, Naples, Sicily, to make sure that each of these was safe, still had no news, so ran for Egypt, only once again Egypt knew nothing of a French fleet—and Egypt's defenses were in so appalling a state one would never have thought she had suffered foreign invasion less than seven years before. Back to Malta again, and only then he learned how Villeneuve had scurried back to Toulon. There was talk, too, of troops, muskets, saddles, being embarked in the enemy fleet—surely it meant that, but for the storm, Villeneuve would have made for Egypt—which was totally unprepared.

Back he beat to his old station, but the waters off Toulon were to see little more of him. At the end of March, Ville-neuve, his first-hand knowledge of the lubberly nature of his fleet overborne by fresh fiery orders from Napoleon, had put to sea again, was sighted on the 31st by two of Nelson's small frigate force and lost again in the night. The French-man met with further luck next day when he fell in with a neutral vessel that told him exactly where Nelson was lying in wait for him. At once he turned away to the west, escaped the trap, approached Cartagena (but the Spanish vessels here were not ready to join him), scudded like a ghost fleet past Gibraltar, came to Cadiz, where one French

117

and six Spanish ships joined him, and then, with a total of eighteen ships, crossed the Atlantic to keep the rendezvous with the other French squadrons. On May 14, he arrived at Martinique.

Nelson had no such luck. For twelve days, having no news of the enemy, he was, in his own words, "entirely adrift." Once more, Villeneuve's destination might be any quarter of the globe, so all that Nelson could do was neither to "go to the eastward of Sicily or the westward of Sardinia, until I know something positive." Not until April 11 could he be sure that the enemy had not sailed eastward, only then could he turn west in pursuit—and still Villeneuve had all the luck. He had had the northeast wind he wanted; Nelson had to fight his way in the teeth of westerly gales so that it took him a month to do what the French had done in nine days. Eventually Gibraltar loomed into sight, but there no more was known than that the enemy had passed through the Straits. After learning this Nelson, who had previously sent warnings to all squadrons threatened by the escape of the enemy, wrote to the Admiralty that he was making for the Scilly Isles. Yet all the while he was growing more convinced that the lost fleet was West Indies bound. If that were so, he considered it his duty to ignore the principle of falling back on western approaches—the West Indies were so important that they must not be left to the mercy of the enemy, and he must go after Villeneuve.

Finally, Nelson's belief was clinched by information given him in Lagos Bay by an old friend, Donald Campbell, now serving in the Portuguese Navy. So the luck turned for Nelson, and the wind veered with it, so that he crossed the Atlantic in ten days fewer than the French; the meeting, however, had other results for poor Campbell, for when it was known that he had talked with Nelson, the French ambassador in Lisbon demanded that he should be dismissed, the spineless Portuguese government yielded, and eventually poor Campbell died in poverty. He had deserved better of his country.

The long chase was on. With eleven ships of the line (and one of them, the *Superb,* a terribly slow sailer) Nelson's aim was to bring to battle a fleet nearly twice the size of his; he told his captains they must each engage a Frenchman, leaving all six Spaniards to him. "When I haul down my colors I expect you to do the same—and not till then."

He had begun the crossing on the evening of May 11; on June 4 he reached Barbados, warned of his coming, and found there two more ships and information—false information that misled him as fatally as he had been misled when Bonaparte had sailed to Egypt. He himself, after much thought had decided that Villeneuve was making for Martinique, and therefore, after touching Barbados, had intended to press on in a northwest direction for this island. However, he was now informed that a certain General Brereton had sent word that the enemy had been seen sailing *south;* this meant that all Nelson's calculations had been wrong, and Villeneuve was making for Tobago and Trinidad. As long as he could, Nelson stuck to his guns, but, as he explained bitterly afterwards, "I could not, in the face of Generals and Admirals, go northwest, when it was *apparently* clear that the enemy had gone south." But he was filled with foreboding. "If your intelligence proves false, you lose me the French fleet," he said.

Picture his fleet, prepared for battle, vainly searching island after island bright in the strong summer light, every vessel expectant as a new island swam into sight—surely the enemy *must* be here! And then incredulous as lookout after lookout chanted, "Nothing . . . nothing . . . nothing . . ." (As lookouts had chanted on two occasions at Alexandria seven years before.)

When at last reliable news was obtained, it nearly broke Nelson's heart—on June 6, the enemy had been sighted off the Saints; he *had* been right, after all, and "if either General Brereton could not have wrote, or his look-out man had been blind, nothing could have prevented my fighting them . . ."

There was little hope of bringing them to battle now. From the northerly course in which they had been seen steering, Nelson guessed they were doubling back to Europe; the fast brig *Curieux* was sent off to warn the Admiralty, and the weary chase was resumed once more. But now all the depression Nelson had known since first losing the enemy settled down on him with redoubled weight—he had so *nearly* come upon them. His diary has some illuminating entries:

"21 *June.* Midnight, nearly calm, saw three planks, which I think came from the French fleet. Very miserable, which is very foolish . . ."

"18 *July.* Cape Spartel in sight, but no French fleet, nor any information about them. How sorrowful this makes me! but I cannot help myself . . ."

"20 *July.* I went on shore (Gibraltar) for the first time since 16 June 1803, and from having my foot out of the *Victory*, two years, wanting ten days . . ."

I think the importance of the last entry can be fully understood only if you have been to Portsmouth and seen the *Victory*. She appears so *tiny* to modern eyes. Nelson, with about eight hundred other human beings, lived in her crowded quarters for close to two years without ever setting foot outside her. Such was the nature of the service he gave to his country.

But he did not expect his country to be grateful, rather he expected to be blamed, never realizing that his mere name had saved the West Indies and a great sugar convoy of two hundred vessels, and ruined Napoleon's careful schemes.

Villeneuve, again luckier in his information, had learned that the dreaded enemy was on his track, and the knowledge made him forget the forty days he should have spent awaiting the other French squadrons and conquering British possessions and capturing convoys. After only twenty-six days, in his fear of Nelson, he dared even to defy Napoleon, and started home—alone.

Napoleon was to be more surprised than were the British by his admiral's abrupt reappearance—the British indeed, expecting the return, sent a fleet to meet the truant. The little *Curieux* had actually sighted the enemy sailing on a course to the north of the Mediterranean, which made it certain that Villeneuve was making for Biscay or Brest to release the other French squadrons. There was a new First Lord of the Admiralty—new, that is, in that particular office, but hardly in service, for he was almost Britain's oldest admiral. Now Lord Barham, on hearing the news brought by the captain of the little brig, took such swift action that Napoleon later refused to believe that an old gentleman of seventy-eight could act with such speed. Nor did his lordship believe in defensive tactics; Sir Robert Calder was to take his own ships, with which he had been watching Ferrol, reinforced by the ships that had watched Rochefort, out into the Atlantic to meet Villeneuve.

Unfortunately, Calder's first aim always was to play safe. He had been that flag-captain to Sir John Jervis who had thought Nelson's conduct at St. Vincent absolutely deplorable, for it was risky and against the rules. Now, obeying orders, he duly sailed west and met Villeneuve, but the battle that followed was not a wholehearted affair on his part—though perhaps it is truer to say his *mind* was not wholly engaged; he kept thinking uneasily that the squadrons from the ports his ships had been watching might have discovered that the British vessels had gone, they *might* come up and take him in the rear . . . Scarcely the frame of mind necessary for victory, and, as a matter of fact, Calder's salvation lay in the fact that if *he* were afraid of an enemy force appearing at his back, Villeneuve was even more appalled at the thought that the vengeful Nelson was hot on his heels.

The encounter commenced at 5 p.m. on July 22, and two of Villeneuve's ships were captured; on July 23, the two fleets kept each other in sight, but did not renew the fighting; on July 24, they parted company, Calder going off north to join Cornwallis, Villeneuve making first for Vigo, then for Ferrol, which he reached on August 1. He was deeply depressed. His fleet, he said, was frightful. His own ships had gone to sea with "bad masts, bad sails, bad rigging," the Spanish ships should never have gone to sea at all. Most of the crews were sick, the captains had little experience of fighting—even of being at sea—and all they could do in the way of tactics was to follow the ship ahead of them. All their drill had been done at anchor; their gunnery practice, because that had been in harbor too, had been with blank cartridges, so this lack of fighting efficiency was scarcely surprising, while another defect—low morale—was also to be expected. Being on the run, as this fleet had been from the moment it left Toulon, is never good for the nerve.

Yet if, in both crossings of the Atlantic, the most anxious glances in Villeneuve's ships had been cast astern, for the sight of British topsails on the horizon, at Boulogne the army was watching hopefully night and day for the sight of Villeneuve's own fleet; Napoleon himself rode along the sand every morning and gazed to sea with his spyglass, but all in vain. He never came. At Ferrol he had found awaiting him a message from Napoleon written in mid-July repeating that he was to "maneuver in such a way as to render us masters of the Strait of Dover," but if this were impossible, he was to make for Cadiz.

Napoleon should never have offered Villeneuve this loophole. If he put to sea again, and steered northwest, he would meet Cornwallis, and somewhere in the Atlantic, drawing closer every day, was Nelson. To go north meant running into a trap; Cadiz meant shelter. To that shelter he raced now, with British squadrons from the north after him. Outside Cadiz was Collingwood with three ships; Villeneuve tried to destroy the little squadron, but Collingwood twisted and turned like an eel, and then, when the enemy gave up in disgust and entered Cadiz, Collingwood went back on guard. This was on August 20; two days later Collingwood received reinforcements of four ships; on the 30th, eighteen. Napoleon's dream of invading England was over.

Some days before, he had been writing to Villeneuve, hopefully sending the letter to Brest, "England is ours . . . Appear for forty-eight hours, and all will be ended." But by this time he, too, was casting glances over his shoulder; Britain's ally, Austria, was arming, and if Villeneuve did not appear soon, the Army of England would turn east and march on Vienna. Villeneuve did not come, and on September 2, Napoleon left Boulogne to chastise Austria that had dared to defy him again.

On that same day, September 2, Nelson learned that Villeneuve was at Cadiz. He had been spending a brief leave at home; this news meant that leave—his last—was over. On September 15, he was at sea in the *Victory* once more.

Hero of Trafalgar

Lord Nelson had saluted Cornwallis' flag off Ushant on August 15, but had received a signal to go on up-Channel towards Portsmouth, which he reached three days later. The "leave" was spent mostly in London, consulting with members of the government, who lost little time in telling him his services would soon be required again. (Charles Lamb saw him walking in Pall Mall, and wrote, "I have followed him in fancy ever since . . . looking just as a hero should look.")

In a private conversation, Nelson described to Captain

Keats how he would attack the enemy . . .

"I shall go at them at once, if I can, about one-third of their line from their leading ship . . . What do you think of it . . ? I'll tell you what *I* think of it. I think it will surprise and confound the enemy. They won't know what I am about. It will bring forward a pell-mell battle, and that is what I want."

But at the time that he spoke, no one knew where Villeneuve had gone, and anxiety was mingled with uncertainty, for it *was* known that a great British convoy, homeward-bound from India, was coming up past Portugal and Biscay, and it was feared Villeneuve might be lying in wait for it. As we know, all Villeneuve wanted was the shelter of Cadiz, but had he indeed attacked the convoy, the history of the entire world would have been different, for one of the passengers was a young general thirty-six years old.

Two days after landing, this same young soldier made his way to the Colonial Office, gave his name, explained why he had come, and was asked to wait in a small room just off the entrance hall. He was to wait there for some considerable time, but if you think it extraordinary enough that the most promising of Britain's younger generals should be left to kick his heels for more than an hour, you will think it even more extraordinary that, sharing his vigil, was the man universally regarded as the greatest sailor that had ever served the country. There in the anteroom, also condemned to wait, was Nelson—the young Irishman might have been out of the country for nine years, but he had read enough about him to recognize him at once. Nelson, although from past bitter experience he regarded most military men as stupid in the extreme, began chatting to the newcomer (one feels he must have been so bored he welcomed any companion in distress), but almost immediately the terse replies of his scarlet-coated fellow sufferer gave him a pleasant shock, being marked by good sense and keen intelligence. Nelson, intrigued, made an excuse, and slipped away to discover the identity of the brown-faced young officer. The name Sir Arthur Wellesley made many things clear to him, for by a fiery attack against tremendous odds the young man had won a quite astonishing victory. Army officer or not, *he* could be treated as an equal, and this Nelson on his return to the waiting room proceeded to do. The minutes raced past, an hour had gone, but Arthur Wellesley no longer resented having to wait. He listened, fascinated, to his companion's discussion of world affairs, and when eventually, it was announced that the minister was free to see Lord Nelson, young General Wellesley was left like a man waking from a dream, when the world of reality seems sadly lacking in color and life.

Thus, in a dingy little waiting room in Downing Street, on Thursday, September 12, 1805, the future Duke of Wellington, at the beginning of the long march to Waterloo, met for the only time Nelson, almost at the end of his laborious cruise.

That end was very close now. For almost a fortnight it had been known that Villeneuve was at Cadiz. Blackwood, the brilliant young frigate captain, had brought the dispatches to London, and had called on the way to tell Nelson. It was five in the morning, but Nelson was up. He read the news in the visitor's face. "I am sure you bring me news of the French and Spanish fleets!" he exclaimed, and when Blackwood had given the details, he said, "Depend on it, Blackwood, I shall yet give Mr. Villeneuve a drubbing."

Then at half past ten on the evening of the day after he had talked with Arthur Wellesley, Nelson left his home for the last time. In his diary he wrote, "May the great God, Whom I adore, enable me to fulfil the expectations of my country . . . If it is His good providence to cut short my days upon earth, I bow with the greatest submission."

Early on the morning of the 14th, he reached Portsmouth, and, after doing what business had to be done on shore, he made his way to the beach. Such a great concourse of people had gathered to look their last on him that he left the inn by the back door and sought his barge by an unexpected route. But the people were not to be denied. They found him, surrounded him—but this was no ordinary crowd. These people knelt weeping on the cobble stones, and cried blessings on his name.

In his barge, Nelson said quietly to Hardy that once he had had their cheers, but now he had their hearts. There was no exaggeration in what he said. To only one other person in English history has equal love and trust been given, and that is the only monarch called "the Great." Alfred's people called him "England's Darling"; Nelson, descendant of those Danes against whom Alfred had warred, might well share that name.

On September 28, he joined the fleet waiting outside Cadiz, clasped once more the hand of his oldest and dearest friend, Collingwood, now his second-in-command, and on the next day celebrated his forty-seventh birthday. One by one the captains of his fleet came aboard the flagship to pay their respects; too often we fall into the mistake of thinking that they also were old friends, tried comrades, that Nelson, as it were, sailed the Seven Seas from the Battle of the Nile onwards with a permanent escort of the same ships, captains and crews. Nothing would be less like the truth; most of these men were strangers to him—yet such was the magic of his name that the fleet had gone wild with joy at the thought that he had come to lead them, and captains going to greet a new admiral, instead of saluting stiffly, and being very formal and correct, grinned their delight, forgetting his rank, so Nelson wrote happily, "in the enthusiasm with which they greeted me." Yet the fact remained that most of the officers were strangers, that September was nearly spent when he took over command, and that he *must* fight Villeneuve soon if he was to fight him at all, for soon the terrible autumn gales would make it impossible to keep his fleet close to Cadiz. (Such a gale was to arise as darkness fell on the day of Trafalgar, and cause indescribable damage.) So he had to train his captains in a matter of days, train them, moreover, to win an entirely new kind of battle, the kind he had won at the Nile—"not victory, but conquest," he himself had said—but this had to be won in a brief autumn day. Yet in that short time, as he himself said as he lay dying, he "bargained" for twenty enemy prizes.

What then did he plan to do in this, his last battle—and the only battle in which he held command against an enemy not at anchor? First, he wanted a "close and decisive battle." Secondly, in order to save time, as at the Battle of the Nile, he would not expect his captains to wait for signals. They were to act as they thought best in the circumstances—in other words, use their initiative. Nelson himself had acted as *he* had thought best at Cape St. Vincent and was the last man to think that one law applied to himself alone, and another to everyone else. So captains were to use their own initiative—revolutionary when you remember how rigid a thing is naval discipline—yet, of course, if every captain was allowed to act as he thought best without knowing what Nelson planned to achieve, the result might be sheer chaos. Therefore, Nelson, in the short time left for preparation, must make his captains understand thoroughly what he wanted to do, and then let them achieve that grand result by the actions they thought best (as he himself had carried out Sir John Jervis's plan at St. Vincent.) Nelson's method of working has been summed up in a single sentence: "Nelson did not fight in order to carry out a plan, instead he planned to carry out a fight." With other admirals, it was the other way round.

129

You will remember that Nelson, talking over tactics with Keats on his brief leave, had spoken of a "pell-mell battle," the method by which he planned to get his fleet into action in the shortest possible time. (*Time* was indeed the word he could not forget—so little time left in the fast-dying year in which he might bring Villeneuve to battle, and even if he managed to do this, so little time in a brief October day to clinch a victory.) Certainly there would be no time to organize a single orderly line of battle with ships keeping regular intervals as if taut on an invisible string (the older admirals' delight). But he proposed to do better than this; to get at the enemy even more quickly there would be not one British attack, but two, one division under Collingwood attacking the enemy rear, the other, Nelson's own, attacking the enemy center, and making every effort to capture the enemy commander-in-chief, his flagship being the nerve-center of the combined fleets. While all this was going on, of course, the enemy vanguard could do nothing—a long interval must pass before it could swing about and come to the aid of its comrades. In other words, as at the Nile, Nelson would so maneuver that the battle would really be won before ever a shot was fired—and again a good third of the enemy would be helpless spectators of the destruction of the rest.

He called his captains to him and explained what he called *The Nelson Touch*. They were ecstatic. "It must succeed!" they repeated. "It must succeed." Again their enthusiasm made them forget formality. They said, "You are, my lord, surrounded by friends whom you inspire with confidence."

It was far different with poor Villeneuve. In Cadiz was no friendship, no confidence—only sickness, and shortage of money, supplies, weapons. All that the combined fleets had abundance of was quarrels. On October 8, Villeneuve held a council of war which almost ended with French and Spaniards at each other's throats. All that the officers could agree upon was "that the vessels of both nations were for the most part badly equipped, that a portion of the crews had never been trained at sea, and that, in short, the fleet was not in a state to perform the services appointed to it." (The new orders sent by Napoleon when he had given up the idea of invading England that year involved breaking into the Mediterranean and landing troops at Naples.) It did not seem as if Nelson would get his battle.

But time was all-important for Villeneuve also, if only he had known it; for him, too, the sands were fast running out. Another admiral was being sent from Paris to supersede him, by October 10 he was at Madrid, and finally Villeneuve's slow-kindling recklessness would be alight. He would not wait tamely to be relieved of his command, to be branded as a coward; he would take his fleet to sea before his successor set foot in Cadiz. On October 19, he made the signal, "Make sail and proceed."

Nelson was fifty miles to the west-southwest of Cadiz, but Blackwood's frigate, *Euryalus*, was so close that morning that from her decks might be seen the ripple of the wave on the beach, or caught the morning fragrance coming off the land. At six the morning sun showed the watchers the enemy emerging one by one from the harbor mouth; up soared the signal flags—the signal for which they had all been praying—"Enemy's ships coming out of port." It was passed along the line of ships stretching across the horizon to westward, each just within sight of the next, so that messages could flicker from masthead to masthead. Within two hours Nelson knew that his supreme chance had come.

But two days must pass before he could seize that chance, and in that time he and his fleet thought that again the enemy had been lost. The British had, in fact, overestimated the seamanship of their foes, and had reasoned that any fleet

131

beginning to leave harbor at six in the morning should be at sea that same day; actually it took all that time for only one division to grope its way out, and not until noon on the 20th was the entire enemy fleet at sea. It numbered thirty-three sail of the line; Nelson had twenty-seven.

Once the enemy was at sea, Nelson's task was a tricky one. All the signs pointed to an enemy attempt to get into the Mediterranean, which must be prevented of course, yet, at the same time, it would not do to let Villeneuve sight Nelson's main fleet too soon. He had found the nerve to put to sea; whether he would *stay* at sea once he had sighted the British battle fleet was a different matter. So Nelson kept out of sight, and Blackwood and the frigates shadowed the enemy—on this occasion Nelson had no need to complain of his frigate force—and only after nightfall on the 20th, when it was too late for the enemy to run back to Cadiz, was the horizon lit by the blue signal lights of the British fleet. The 21st dawned grey, heavy with cloud. The cold early light showed a cape rising from the haze to the east—Trafalgar. A steady swell was coming in from the Atlantic; a light wind blew from the northwest. The enemy was ten to twelve miles away.

Nelson was on deck at daybreak, but shortly afterwards he went below, and made the last entry in his notebook:

"May the Great God, Whom I worship, grant to my Country, and for the benefit of Europe in general, a great and glorious Victory; and may no misconduct in anyone tarnish it; and may humanity after Victory be the predominant feature in the British Fleet. For myself, individually, I commit my life to Him Who made me, and may His blessing light upon my endeavors for serving my Country faithfully. To Him I resign myself and the just cause which is entrusted to me to defend. Amen. Amen. Amen."

Then he went back up on deck, and made signal to form line of battle in two divisions. Now the Nelson touch was to be put into action.

Once any idea has proved successful, it is only too easy to say, "How obvious! Why did no one think of it before?" But try to see Nelson's plan of attacking in two headlong divisions, in place of one stately line parallel with the enemy, as something quite unheard of, and then you will have a chance of recapturing the sheer *excitement* of Trafalgar, the ecstasy of veteran captains who had been like schoolboys when the plan had been explained to them. Trafalgar was utterly unlike all past battles; let me illustrate the difference by a quotation: "He (Nelson) looked upon them (former engagements), we may assume, as contests between two one-armed boxers, and so far as he was concerned, he intended to fight with two arms. His fleet was to have a left punch and a right punch." Hence, of course, the two divisions, his own and Collingwood's, but there was far more to the Nelson Touch than this. It meant blitzing the enemy, striking like lightning. The enemy, Nelson had told Keats, pacing up and down in his garden, "won't know what I am about." They would be waiting for him to form lines, instead of going for them pell-mell.

Yet perhaps the most astounding feature of the Battle of Trafalgar is the fact that though the Nelson Touch amazed Nelson's own officers, one man was *not* surprised, and that man was—Villeneuve. With astonishing accuracy he prophesied before putting to sea exactly what Nelson would do: "The British Fleet will not be formed in a line of battle parallel with the combined fleet . . . Nelson . . . will seek to break our line, envelop our rear . . ." But he made no suggestion as to how his own fleet was to counter this unheard-of mode of attack; probably he asked himself despairingly what was the use! Had he not said that it was capable of

carrying out only one maneuver, that of forming line ahead
—*which was exactly what Nelson wanted?*

During the American Civil War, when the great soldier
of the Confederacy, Robert E. Lee, seemed invincible, the
soldiers of the armies sent against him, having no faith in
their own leaders, said there was one general for both armies,
and that was Bobby Lee, for both armies did exactly what
he wanted. The same bitter comment might have been made
by Villeneuve and his officers about Nelson. But make no
mistake on one all-important point; however hopeless the
French and Spaniards might believe their cause to be, they
all, from admirals down, fought with the utmost gallantry
and resolution.

And Nelson himself? Previously he had reveled in the
heat of battle, but on this occasion, though he was very
cheerful, and his courage was flawless, there was none of that
exhilaration so noticeable at the Nile and Copenhagen. There
was a strange finality in all he said and did; he told Blackwood, when giving him his final orders, that he would never
see him again; he had said things the day before that could
only mean he did not think he would survive the fighting.

We know the signal he made to his fleet, the most famous
of all signals: "England expects that every man will do his
duty." Napoleon, one of the most ungenerous of enemies,
was to pay Nelson a remarkable compliment a few months
later by ordering that, "France expects that every man will
do his duty," should be painted prominently in every warship
left to him. But the signal had originally commenced, "Nelson confides," and had been altered at the suggestion of the
flag-lieutenant, Pascoe, so that it might be transmitted more
easily. One cannot help regretting the change. Nelson's
magic was always personal; Nelson was ever trustful. But the
altered signal was made, and greeted with cheers. "Now,"
said Nelson quietly, "I can do no more."

Next followed another very famous incident—the attempt to get Nelson to change his coat, covered as it was with decorations, or at least to cover those decorations, for it was known that the French ships carried sharpshooters, who would keep a special lookout for the British admiral. Nelson refused to do either of these things, and said there was not time to go below and change his coat. But this was no answer to the second request, for it would have taken no time at all to have covered his decorations.

You will find that if you become deeply interested in any historical personage, the more you study him and read his letters and diaries, the more you get inside his skin, and feel for him, with him, and, eventually, *as* him. Now I know very well that if I myself were covered with decorations, and there, at terribly short range, were the sharpshooters in the enemy tops, ready to pick me off, I should lose no time in covering the decorations that made me so conspicuous a target. *But one couldn't if one were Nelson.* For him, covering his decorations would mean something quite different from showing ordinary common sense, quite different and far, far worse. It would mean taking off the insignia of honor to save his life. Life saved on such terms would never be sweet to him; in any case, he simply could not do such a thing, any more than he could have hauled down *Victory's* flag in the face of the enemy.

As the two fleets drew nearer, the sun, rising, shone full on the enemy. The British crews took a good look, but with no alarm; their chief feeling was that the enemy monsters would make a fine spectacle as prizes at Spithead. In the *Victory* herself, the officers were doing their best to make out which ship carried the enemy commander-in-chief, for Nelson planned to paralyze the enemy by the capture of his opposite number just as a body is paralyzed by a brain injury. Being unable to decide, he eventually made for the biggest ship in sight—if it came to that, the biggest ship in the world, the *Santissima Trinidad.*

But it was Collingwood's division that attacked first. At eleven-thirty Villeneuve had signalled, "Open fire!" (some eighteen minutes before Nelson had signalled, "England expects . . .") It was about a quarter of an hour afterwards that the first shot actually was heard, when a French vessel opened fire on Collingwood's flagship, the *Royal Sovereign,* at a range of just over a quarter of a mile. At the sound of the opening shot, the vessels on both sides hoisted their colors. Collingwood, a brilliant gunnery expert, held his fire until he broke the enemy line astern of the great *Santa Ana,* which he engaged at point-blank range with dreadful effect. Twenty-five minutes later, Nelson himself went into action at the head of his division. The *Victory* ran down the enemy line enduring the fire of vessel after vessel without returning a shot until, at a few minutes after noon, having thoroughly demoralized her opponents, and leaving them completely in the dark as to what part of the line she would attack, she opened fire with a double broadside. Hardy had told Nelson that he could not break the enemy line, which was "closed like a forest," without running aboard one of the ships; Nelson told him to take his choice—it did not signify much. But it mattered a great deal that the vessel his flagship ran on board, just as her own tiller ropes were shot away, was the *Redoubtable,* for she was a two-decker, whose rigging was therefore much lower than that of the *Victory,* coming very close to the quarter-deck where Nelson and Hardy paced side by side—and the rigging was full of sharpshooters.

These were, indeed, her chief weapons, for after firing only one broadside her lower deck gun ports were lowered for fear the British might try to board through them. Because there was no more gunfire from her, and because she carried no flag, twice Nelson ordered the *Victory's* gunners to cease firing on her, believing she had surrendered, but she was still in the fight, and there perched in the mizzen-top no more than fifteen yards from the *Victory's* quarter-deck were the sharpshooters, one of whom fired the shot that killed Nelson.

Just after half past one, Hardy realized that he had taken the last step alone. He turned, just in time to see Nelson falling from his knees to his left side. A sergeant of Marines and two seamen ran to raise him; in the next instant Hardy was bending over him to hear a faint voice whispering, "Hardy, they have done for me at last . . . my backbone is shot through."

With his own hand Nelson took out his handkerchief and covered his face as the seamen carried him down the ladder —the crew must not know he was hurt—and in the crowded nightmare of the cockpit he insisted on waiting his turn, as he had done at the Battle of the Nile, when he had also thought he was dying. But this time there was to be no reprieve, though he was condemned to linger on in great pain and great thirst for three hours and a quarter amid darkness and the sickly smell of blood and the cries of the wounded. Sometimes, too, there was the shout of "Fire," dreaded by all sailors, even if they had not seen the destruction of the flagship of another mortally wounded admiral seven years before; but his chief anxiety was to see Hardy, and when Hardy did not come, Nelson feared that he, too, was dead.

Hardy, of course, was on deck, fighting, but the dying admiral asked for him repeatedly, not for any selfish reason, but, because in the midst of all his pain he had not lost his passionate devotion to duty. Only Hardy could tell him if the plan of attack was succeeding. His ardent brain still tried to grapple with the responsibilities and problems of high command, even in his agony—but the pain did not matter so much, for it was no new experience to Nelson after thirty-five years at sea. What made it so terribly hard to think down there in the dark cockpit was the regular crash of his flagship's broadsides, so that her dying admiral whispered to her, "Oh, *Victory, Victory,* how you distract my brain!"

But at last Hardy came picking his way between the dead and the dying, and took Nelson's hand. Ten enemy ships had struck, he said. The reaction came fiercely—had any British ships struck? No fear of that, said Hardy, in his deep westcountry voice. Having dealt with the most important matter, Nelson turned to personal affairs. He was going fast, he said, it would all be over soon. Hardy tried to speak hopefully, but Nelson repeated that his backbone was shot through.

When Hardy had gone back on deck, the dying man whispered to the surgeon that the pain was so great that he wished he was dead. Yet, he added wistfully, one would like to live a little longer too.

A little longer even in such pain—if he might hear from Hardy that the victory he had planned was indeed won. And Hardy, who had never failed him, did not fail him now. Within an hour he came stooping through the shambles of the cockpit, took Nelson's hand in his, and congratulated him on having gained a complete victory. At least fourteen or fifteen ships had struck. Nelson whispered that he had bargained for twenty and then said perhaps the most important of all the things he said as he lay dying, important, because it shows firstly, his seamanship, secondly, the sense of duty that made his chief thought, even now, the safety of his ships. The swell coming steadily in from the Atlantic in the morning had given ominous warning of an approaching storm. "*Anchor,* Hardy, *anchor!*" said Nelson.

After that he seemed to drift away on waves of delirium. Hardy stood up, knowing he must hasten up on deck again to direct the fight, but knowing also that he would never see his admiral alive again. He was a typical undemonstrative

Englishman, loathing any great display of feeling, but now he knelt down again, unbidden, and kissed Nelson's forehead. The action recalled the dying man a little. "Who is that?" he whispered.

"It is Hardy."

"God bless you, Hardy."

Hardy went away; Nelson whispered, "I wish I had not left the deck."

Death was coming fast, and he could speak only with great difficulty now, but he was heard to repeat, many times, "Thank God I have done my duty!" and, at the very end, "God and my country!"

He died at about half past four. As the early October dusk fell on the triumphant British fleet and their eighteen prizes, no Admiral's lights glimmered aboard the *Victory*.

The feeling of the fleet he had commanded was summed up in the sentence the young lieutenant sent home with the tidings of Trafalgar:

"Sir, we have gained a great victory, but we have lost Lord Nelson!"

The whole nation shared that feeling of loss. We are told that complete strangers, meeting in the streets, would stop to say, "We have lost Nelson!"

But blind Milton, many years before, describing the glorious death of another sightless hero who, dying, had destroyed the enemies of his country, had written the best epitaph for Nelson:

> "Nothing is here for tears, nothing to wail
> Or knock the breast; no weakness, no contempt,
> Dispraise or blame; nothing but well and fair
> And what may quiet us in a death so noble."

Index of Place Names

Africa, 58
Aboukir, 43
Aboukir Bay, 80, 95, 115
Aboukir Island, 80
Alexandria, 74, 75, 76, 77, 119
America, 17
American mainland, 33
Americas, the, 59
Amiens, 105
Antipodes, the, 115
Archipelago, 75
Asia Minor, 76
Atlantic, 17, 30, 50, 118, 121, 122, 123, 132
Atlantic, South, 58
Austerlitz, 75
Austria, 68, 123
Baltic, the, 37, 89, 91, 95, 104
Barbados, 22, 119
Bastia, 40
Bath, 66
Biscay, 121, 126
Boulogne, 107, 116, 122, 123
Brest, 107, 108, 116, 121, 123
Britain, 32, 46, 89, 91, 105, 110, 121, 123, 126
Burnham Thorpe, 24
Cadiz, 47, 50, 54, 55, 58, 108, 109, 116, 117, 123, 126, 127, 128, 129, 130, 131, 132
Cairo, 76
Calvi, 40
Canada, 30
Canary Islands, 58
Cape of Good Hope, 25
Cape St. Vincent, 50, 58, 61, 84, 121, 129
Cape Spartel, 120
Cartagena, 47, 108, 116, 117

Central America, 28
Channel, the, 37, 107, 108, 109, 110, 116, 125
Channel Islands, 70
Chatham, 19, 23
Copenhagen, 94, 95, 134
Corsica, 39, 40, 46, 47, 59, 71
Crete, 75
Danish coast, 30
Dardanelles, the, 76
Dead Sea, 87
Denmark, 91, 103, 105
Dorset, 47
Dover, Strait of, 123
Downing Street, 127
East Indies, 25
Egypt, 74, 75, 76, 77, 87, 89, 116, 117, 119
Elba, 47
Elsinore, 95
England, 17, 25, 31, 32, 34, 35, 37, 41, 51, 57, 76, 87, 94, 107, 123, 128, 131, 134, 136
Europe, 58, 68, 95, 110, 113, 120, 132
Ferrol, 108, 121, 122
Fiorenzo Bay, 45
France, 23, 28, 31, 35, 70, 72, 76, 77, 105, 110, 115, 116
France, Southern, 113
Gibraltar, 45, 70, 105, 117, 118, 120
Gibraltar, Strait of, 50, 118
Gloucestershire, 70
Greece, 76
Greenland, 17
Gronenburg Castle, 94
Gulf of Lyons, 71
Hanover Square, 66
Iceland, 17
India, 25, 74, 126

Ireland, 44, 68
Italy, 43, 46, 68, 73, 88
Jamaica, 28, 29
King's Channel, 96
Lagos Bay, 118
Leeward Islands, 32, 34
Levant, the, 76
Lisbon, 118
London, 19, 23, 33, 66,
    106, 110, 125
Low Countries, the, 108
Lynn, 19
Lyons, Gulf of, 71
Madrid, 131
Malta, 39, 74, 75, 89, 107,
    110, 117
Martinique, 118, 119
Mediterranean, 17, 22, 30,
    37, 39, 41, 42, 45, 46, 67,
    68, 76, 87, 88, 89, 107,
    113, 114, 115, 121, 131,
    132
Medway, the, 15, 19, 20
Mexico, 58
Middle Ground, the, 96
Mosquito Coast, 29
Naples, 68, 73, 74, 87, 88,
    89, 117, 131
New York, 30
Nile, 37, 44, 100, 128, 129,
    130, 134, 137
Nore, the, 23
Norfolk, 24, 35, 36
North Country, the, 28
North Sea, the, 24, 30, 89,
    93
Pall Mall, 125
Paris, 106, 116, 131
Portsmouth, 105, 120, 125,
    128
Portugal, 68, 126
Pyramids, the, 76
Riviera, the, 113
Riviera coast, 43
Rochefort, 108, 121
Rosetta, 86
Russia, 91, 104, 105

St. Fiorenzo, 40
St. George's Church, 66
St. Vincent, Cape, 50, 58,
    61, 84, 121, 129
Saints, the, 120
San Juan River, 29
Santa Cruz de Teneriffe,
    58, 59, 61, 62, 65
Sardinia, 117, 118
Sardinian harbor, a, 71
Scilly Isles, 118
Seven Seas, the, 128
Sicily, 76, 89, 117, 118
South America, 28
South American continent,
    29
Southern France, 113
Spain, 28, 36, 41, 46, 59,
    107, 108
Spithead, 135
Strait of Dover, 123
Strait of Gibraltar, 50
Sweden, 91
Swedish shore, 95
Syracuse, 76, 77
Syria, 76
Teneriffe, Santa Cruz de,
    58, 59, 61, 62, 65
Texel, 108
Thames, 22
Tobago, 119
Toulon, 42, 44, 47, 68, 70,
    73, 106, 107, 108, 110,
    114, 115, 116, 117, 122
Tower, the, 23
Trafalgar, 37, 43, 50, 75,
    107, 129, 132, 133, 139
Trinidad, 119
Ushant, 108, 125
Vienna, 123
Vigo, 122
Waterloo, 75, 127
West Indies, 17, 22, 28, 30,
    31, 33, 36, 46, 50, 109,
    116, 118, 120
Westminster Abbey, 56
Yarmouth, 92

141

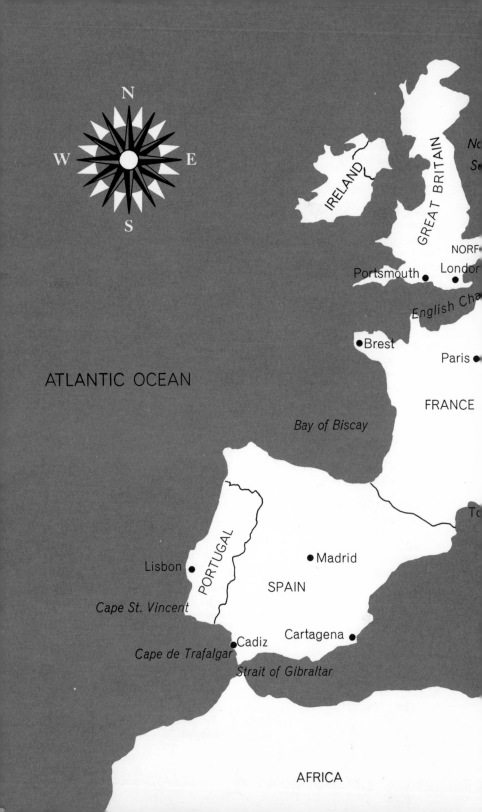